Quest for the Enlighte

"I loved Anna's book. As someone also on a spiritual journey, I welcomed her openness and honesty when describing the highs and the lows of this journey—the intense experience of love and light and, at the same time, the bruising and painful struggles with her ego in its many manifestations. Anna was not afraid to plough her own furrow, turning away from a conventional life and truly honouring what it means to search for her truth. In that journey, Anna finds compassion for herself and the world and a deep and enduring sense of peace and presence that lies in the background of awareness, waiting to be noticed and enjoyed—a context within which suffering no longer holds her in its thrall."

~ **Rachel Lebus,** psychotherapist and mindfulness meditation teacher

"Initiated by a life-changing dream, Anna abandons all that is familiar, to follow her inner calling. Eventually, she discovers Tara, the feminine aspect of Tibetan Buddhism, and embarks on a pilgrimage to understand this deity in all of her aspects. This healing journey eventually brings her home. Told in a compelling, unsparingly honest and contemporary way, this is a woman's story of journeying into the heart of the divine, through the Tibetan Buddhist teachings and through discovering Tara. Clear and insightful as she shares her longings and vulnerability, this is a spiritual quest for our times, when the reemergence of the feminine is what is needed to heal and transform our crisis-ridden world. This book is a companion, a guide, a support, and a reminder of the living presence of the divine within us all."

~ **Dr. Sara Trevelyan,** psychotherapist, interfaith minister, and author of *Freedom Found*

"This is a wonderful and informative book. Anna teaches us that Christianity and Buddhism are not mutually exclusive but are complements of each other. The author writes in such an honest and fresh manner that cannot fail to delight her readers. A must for anyone seeking a spiritual path. I didn't want to put this book down."

~ **Lolai O'Dwyer,** sales manager and mother

"*Quest for the Enlightened Feminine* is the engaging and entertaining recounting of one woman's path towards enlightenment. Her pursuit of higher spiritual understanding has been punctuated by tough challenges, deep disappointments, and times of fundamental realization and profound insight as her path guided a constant expansion of her consciousness. I found the book a fascinating read and learned a lot from it. And, of course, such a journey never really ends."

~ **Peter Rhodes-Dimmer,** retired international businessman and author of *The Human Journey*

"The spiritual quest—when it arises, it can become a driving passion, often with many challenges. Anna Howard, in this personal narrative, shares with us the agonies and ecstasies she has encountered along her particular path. The spiritual journey indeed varies for all of us, and I have found this book a heart-warming read, inspiring, and reminding me of my own spiritual unfoldings."

~ **Kenneth Ray Stubbs, Ph.D.,** author of *The Essential Tantra*

Quest for the Enlightened Feminine

Faith, Tara, and the Path of Compassion

Anna Howard

FINDHORN PRESS

Findhorn Press
One Park Street
Rochester, Vermont 05767
www.findhornpress.com

Findhorn Press is a division of Inner Traditions International

Disclaimer
The information in this book is given in good faith and intended for information only. Neither author nor publisher can be held liable by any person for any loss or damage whatsoever which may arise from the use of this book or any of the information therein.

A CIP record for this title is available from the Library of Congress

ISBN 979-8-88850-142-9 (print)
ISBN 979-8-88850-143-6 (ebook)

Printed and bound in the United States by Lake Book Manufacturing, LLC

10 9 8 7 6 5 4 3 2 1

Illustrations: see p. 244; except for p. 13 © Kagyu Samye Dzong Brussels
Edited by Nicky Leach
Text design and layout by Anna-Kristina Larsson
This book was typeset in Garamond, Bodega Serif and Spartan

To send correspondence to the author of this book, mail a first-class letter to the author c/o Inner Traditions • Bear & Company, One Park Street, Rochester, VT 05767, USA and we will forward the communication, or contact the author directly at **www.white-tara.co.uk**.

This book is dedicated to my mother and father—

Gone beyond but forever here

A share of this book's royalties will be donated to
The Akong Memorial Foundation and to Bodhicharya.

Contents

Part Two

Tara and the Peace Pilgrimage

Foreword

When I arrived in Scotland in 1969, I was a rebel on the run, a restless and confused young man who found it difficult to adapt to life at Samye Ling Monastery. Samye Ling was the first Tibetan Buddhist Centre in the West, founded two years earlier by my brother Akong Rinpoche and one of my teachers and friends, Trungpa Rinpoche. Samye Ling was a far cry from the monasteries I had known in Tibet and very scruffy compared to His Holiness the Karmapa's monastery at Rumtek in Sikkim, where I had been living.

It took me a long time to realize that, if I really wanted happiness and to make those I loved proud of me, I had to change. After years of resisting the teachings and practices that my life was immersed in—the means to bring about the changes I knew were needed—I decided it was time. To everyone's surprise, and within a very short period of time, I had taken life ordination as a gelong monk and had embarked on a long retreat in Woodstock, New York, in the United States.

By the time I became abbot of Samye Ling, the Dharma and my devotion and commitment to practice had brought about a radical transformation. I could see the struggles and unhappiness that seemed to blight the lives of Westerners, despite the material comforts they enjoyed, and understood the confusion that arose with an unbridled embrace of the many attractions and distractions on offer.

I wanted to help them. I wanted to create opportunities for them to experience the same benefits of the Dharma I had been given, and which my brother Akong was seeking to provide. For me, that meant finding ways to allow Westerners to take ordination; the stability, discipline, structure, and purpose afforded by the robes was something I wanted to make available for others.

It took me a while to realize that this was a lot to ask of young Westerners with no previous history or experience of Buddhism or the Tibetan culture. Those early years were wonderful in many ways, but nowadays I take a more pragmatic approach to ordination and monastic vows.

I welcome Anna's honest and revealing account of her experience as a Western laywoman encountering the teachings of Tibetan Buddhism for the first time and the struggles she went through. There were often greater challenges for women wanting to study Buddhism, certainly historically, as the Tibetan culture was, and still is, very traditional. Women were expected to become good wives and mothers rather than nuns or teachers.

We have a female Buddha in our tradition known as Tara, whose story is often a source of inspiration and encouragement for women. Tara is seen as the mother of all the Buddhas and is widely revered and loved throughout Tibet by laypeople and monastics, men and women alike. Despite the rocky nature of the connection between the author and myself in the early years, she took a strong interest in Tara and the Dharma and was a determined student. As with so many other young people living at Samye Ling at that time, there were many ups and downs—we were all learning together.

Integrating Tibetan Buddhism into Western culture will take time. There is ongoing debate about how much it should adapt in order to become more palatable for Westerners and how much it should seek to preserve the traditional ways in which Tibetan Buddhism is taught and practised. I see this book as an interesting and important example of how integration can happen. It is heart-warming to see how Christianity and Buddhism can complement one another and both support the development of compassion and wisdom within the mind. Spiritual development is the bedrock of human happiness and wellbeing, as I see it, and religious differences need not be an obstacle.

I hope everyone who reads this book will receive great benefit. Spanning over 30 years of adult life, it offers insights and inspiration for those who may be looking for spiritual direction, practical tools to help navigate the everyday chattering monkey mind, and a very human story of hope and self-discovery.

Choje Lama Yeshe Losal Rinpoche

Choje Lama Yeshe Losal Rinpoche is abbot of Kagyu Samye Ling Monastery and Tibetan Centre in Scotland, chairman of Rokpa Trust, and executive director of the Holy Isle Project.

༄༅། །རྗེ་བཙུན་སྒྲོལ་མ་ལ་འདོད་དོན་གསོལ་འདེབས།

Prayer to Jetsün Tārā for the Fulfilment of Wishes

*by Jetsün Drakpa Gyaltsen**

རྗེ་བཙུན་བཅོམ་ལྡན་འདས་མ་ཐུགས་རྗེ་ཅན། །
Noble and compassionate Tārā, we pray to you:
བདག་དང་མཐའ་ཡས་སེམས་ཅན་ཐམས་ཅད་ཀྱི། །
May I and all sentient beings, infinite in number,
སྒྲིབ་གཉིས་བྱང་ཞིང་ཚོགས་གཉིས་མྱུར་རྫོགས་ནས། །
Purify the two obscurations and swiftly perfect the two accumulations,
རྫོགས་པའི་སངས་རྒྱས་ཐོབ་པར་མཛད་དུ་གསོལ། །
And in so doing may we gain perfect enlightenment.

དེ་མ་ཐོབ་ཀྱི་ཚེ་རབས་ཀུན་དུ་ཡང་། །
Until then, in all our lives,
ལྷ་དང་མི་ཡི་བདེ་བ་མཆོག་ཐོབ་ནས། །
May we find supreme happiness among gods and human beings,
ཐམས་ཅད་མཁྱེན་པ་སྒྲུབ་པར་བྱེད་པ་ལ། །
And may all obstacles to the attainment of omniscience,
བར་ཆད་གདོན་བགེགས་རིམས་དང་ནད་ལ་སོགས། །
As well as harmful influences and disease,

དུས་མིན་འཆི་བར་གྱུར་པ་སྣ་ཚོགས་དང་། །
All that brings untimely death,
རྨི་ལམ་ངན་དང་མཚན་མ་ངན་པ་དང་། །
All bad dreams and evil omens,
འཇིགས་པ་བརྒྱད་སོགས་ཉེ་བར་འཚེ་བ་རྣམས། །
The eight major fears and all forms of harm,
མྱུར་དུ་ཞི་ཞིང་མེད་པར་མཛད་དུ་གསོལ། །
All be swiftly pacified and eliminated.

འཇིག་རྟེན་འཇིག་རྟེན་ལས་ནི་འདས་པ་ཡི། །
May auspiciousness, happiness and prosperity,
བཀྲ་ཤིས་བདེ་ལེགས་ཕུན་སུམ་ཚོགས་པ་རྣམས། །
Both worldly and transcendent,
འཕེལ་ཞིང་རྒྱས་པའི་དོན་རྣམས་མ་ལུས་པ། །
Flourish and expand, and may all our wishes
འབད་མེད་ལྷུན་གྱིས་གྲུབ་པར་མཛད་དུ་གསོལ། །
Be effortlessly and spontaneously fulfilled.

སྒྲུབ་ལ་བརྩོན་ཞིང་དམ་ཆོས་འཕེལ་བ་དང་། །
May we endeavour in the practice, may the Dharma spread,
རྟག་ཏུ་ཁྱེད་སྒྲུབ་ཞལ་མཆོག་མཐོང་བ་དང་། །
May we always meditate on you, and behold your perfect face,
སྟོང་ཉིད་དོན་རྟོགས་བྱང་སེམས་རིན་པོ་ཆེ། །
May we realize the nature of emptiness, and
ཡར་ངོའི་ཟླ་ལྟར་འཕེལ་ཞིང་རྒྱས་པར་མཛོད། །
May precious bodhicitta develop and expand, just like the waxing moon.

*This text is extracted from Drakpa Gyaltsen's Four-Maṇḍala Prayer to Tārā (sgrol ma'i gsol 'debs maN+Dal bzhi pa). Jetsün Drakpa Gyaltsen. "Prayer to Jetsün Tārā for the Fulfilment of Wishes." On Lotsawa House. Trans. Rigpa Translations. www.lotsawahouse.org/tibetan-masters/jetsun-drakpa-gyaltsen/tara-prayer-jetsun-chomden.

Preface

Many people have suggested over the years that I write down my story of how and why I gave up everything to pursue enlightenment, and the unexpected and often challenging consequences that arose. I have been reticent, because to write it down means to share very personal experiences in ways that might be construed as self-indulgent, when the very nature of the quest is to reduce the identity with, and clinging to, the ordinary self.

Yet, it occurred to me that it is often easier to relate to a human story than it is to understand abstract spiritual teachings and, if it's true that our basic humanity is the same, then there is perhaps value in inviting others to journey a while in my footsteps—footsteps that became a path that helped me, and that perhaps can help others, to find a way out of suffering and into a life of far greater peace and inner happiness.

This book is one that I hope will benefit anyone who reads it. If it has crossed your path, I trust that there will be something in it that will bring you either inspiration or encouragement. It is a book that I think will appeal to readers questioning life and looking for a more spiritual direction, as well as to readers who are fully committed to their spiritual development and path but who may have encountered difficulties or doubts, or who simply like to meet like-minded friends along the way. Each one of us has a uniquely personal story and path, which no one else can live or walk for us, but we humans thrive in community and sharing our stories can be enriching and supportive.

I have also decided that now is the time to write this book—not because I have fulfilled my original quest to become enlightened but arguably because I haven't! As you read this story, you will come to understand, I hope, why I might say this, and why this gives us all reasons for hope and joy.

May this book be a source of light and blessing in the world. May it bring us all closer to a state of grace, living in harmony and with love for ourselves, each other, and this precious, beautiful, and vulnerable planet.

Wild Edge of Longing

To see the beauty of another,
The truth, goodness and love.
To envy not the way of men but
Follow the ways of gods.

To know the edge of reason, the
Thundering of passion,
To kiss the tears of sadness whispering
Lost love and longing…
And breathe new life, joy, belonging.

To hold a body born of earth and fire
And never hold a moment.
Soft surrender to the waves of bliss
As the hard edge of fear and time
Shatters and dissolves in awe of the
Majesty of the Holy One.

There.

Between you and me. Within you
And me.
That is you and me.
Together. Apart.
One.

Part One

Following the Call

Chapter 1
The Dream

It was a dream, but a dream that changed everything. I don't recall anything particular happening that would trigger such a dream, but I was questioning many things at the time and had become curious about the spiritual dimension of life.

I recall being in a small church, with just a handful of people in the congregation. The organ was playing gentle music whilst a plain-clothed priest prepared bread and wine at the altar. For no apparent reason, the music abruptly changed mid-cadence and, like a magician casting a spell, enveloped me in a dark and very sinister field of energy.

I began to feel a ground-shaking fear unlike anything I had felt before, which only intensified as the priest came towards me bearing a chalice from which I was supposed to drink. In this chalice appeared to be blood—not the healing blood of Christ but rather, a sacrificial blood, one that I felt would steal my very soul were it to pass my lips.

As he came closer I began to shake, and suddenly from the depths of my being cried out, "Save me Jesus." I don't know where these words came from—I was certainly no Evangelical at the time—but they seemed totally natural when encountering the sheer, existential terror that gripped me in that moment.

All of a sudden, directly in front of me, a figure with long hair wearing a beige robe appeared. He had the most compassionate, loving eyes I had ever gazed upon, and there was no doubt in my mind that this was Jesus. As he looked at me, his eyes radiated ever more compassion and love until every cell of my body was filled and saturated. I began to experience more peace and bliss than I'd ever known; it was as if all prayers were answered at once and all sorrows and cares evaporated. As this feeling sank in, so I heard the words: "This is who you really are. This is who everyone really is."

* * *

I woke up. Jesus was gone, and the church and the priest were gone, but the feelings of peace, deep love, and total bliss remained. So strong were these feelings I couldn't leave the house; instead, I needed to stay still and undisturbed and allow this experience to integrate and permeate my being. For three days, my sensitivity was heightened to a degree that felt unsustainable in the "real" world, which felt noisy, busy, and overwhelming to a degree that was almost torture. I remember walking into Woodstock, the small Oxfordshire market town where I lived, and leaning into any wall I passed—anything to ground myself and return to normal functioning.

Gradually the intensity of my vision abated, and my ordinary mind began to return. This was not altogether welcome. I didn't find life easy at the best of times, and was often beset by some emotional travail or another. The temporary respite I'd had from my own mind was a glimpse into another way of being, but as familiar thoughts, feelings, reactions, and memories took hold again, I realized that there was no short-circuiting the work needed to truly become the person, the being, I'd been told I was—and indeed, experienced myself to be.

For a while, I lived with this double reality—half here, half not here. I might understand this now as the coexistence of relative and ultimate reality, as it would be described within Buddhism, but at the time my only frame of reference was a Christian one. The meeting I'd had with Jesus didn't fade like an ordinary dream, however. Something had happened that had changed everything forever. I needed to figure out what that meant and what I was going to do about it. Or so I believed. Doing rather than being was all I knew at that point.

As time passed, a sense of vocation seeded itself within me. The further the experience of peace and oneness receded, the deeper and greater the human longing for its return, and the growing conviction that nothing in this world could ever bring that about.

If Jesus not only knew who I really was but was Himself the full embodiment of this magnificence and capable of transmitting this information, this knowing, then He was the one I had to turn my heart and attention towards. I had to become like Him; to give my life to Him in some meaningful way—a way that would transform my earthly failings and sorrows, or allow me to transcend them, so that the version of myself He'd revealed to me was indeed a living truth that shone into this world with its qualities of total love, compassion, peace.

I sought answers in the Christian Church. I'd often been drawn to monasteries or convents, choosing most years to spend a week on a retreat somewhere. In particular, I felt at home in Burford Priory in Oxfordshire and at St. Mary's on Lindisfarne. Burford was a traditional Benedictine monastery, and St. Mary's was an open Christian centre, but the warmth of hospitality was always a reminder of the nature of Christ. I was welcome, everyone was welcome; not because we were insiders or prospective converts, but because we were accepted as fully as Christ accepted all those He encountered. But if I wanted to give my entire life to this quest, where could I go? Where could I be? Where could I live?

I decided to try living amongst nuns in a convent for a week, but it would be a week of silence and a turning within in a context that supported and encouraged that. I found a convent in Surrey and entered with trepidation and joy.

There was nothing particularly inspiring about this convent, and it had the smell of an institution and religious house, which always put me off somewhat. Was it the worn, tattered sofas and furnishings that exuded a slightly old and stale aroma? Was it years of burning frankincense that seeped into curtains and carpets and left a lingering sweetness that wasn't entirely pleasant but nevertheless focused the mind and turned it towards prayerful matters?

My room was simple and the Daily Office, the Benedictine rhythm of prayer, became my structure for the day. Getting up early for Matins and Lauds was a struggle, and I slept through a few of these, but I enjoyed all the others. As I slipped deeper into silence, I felt held by the structure of the monastic day and by the nuns and the convent itself. Silence unravels. When we enter retreat, we often feel that "the world is too much with us", but it's not easy to put it down. Only by removing ourselves completely and entering a very different way of life is it possible to leave the world behind in any significant way. This is one of the main purposes and values of retreat.

I've often heard people dismiss the value of the more enclosed religious life, seeing it as selfish and disconnected from the suffering of the world. In my experience, it's the opposite: By dropping out of our worldly preoccupations, we enter the inner peace that naturally includes and loves all others as part of the bigger self, and when we come back to the world, we come back with those qualities more readily expressed and available for others. Convents, monasteries, and centres of religious or spiritual focus are not easy places to live, and most communities work hard in every respect to maintain a stable, loving environment that fosters wellbeing and spiritual nourishment for themselves and others. There has undeniably been abuse within religious orders and organizations, and, sadly, continues to be in places, but it would be wrong to assume that they were, or are, closet dens of iniquity as a result.

In the protected confines of the convent, silence was as natural as breathing. Time was dedicated to what is known as the Great Silence or Noble Silence, so it was easy to stop talking. What wasn't so easy was to get beyond the chattering mind. It was so loud! The sounds of the world mask and drown out the noise going on inside our own heads, and perhaps that's why so many people seem to need radio or television constantly playing in the background. Our chattering minds are like tinnitus with thoughts, and when we're not actively thinking, it can be a shock to discover just how busy the mind is of its own accord. Thoughts, feelings, judgements, memories—on and on and on they go, unchosen and out of control.

As I began to realize this, I became quite alarmed and felt increasingly trapped. There was so little space, and these thoughts were unbidden and operating without a thinker. I knew nothing about meditation at this point, and didn't yet have any tools to work constructively with what was being uncovered. So, instead, I found solace through distraction or redirecting my focus. I went for walks in the woods, attended the Offices, read books, and tried to talk to Jesus, finding Him in the many statues around the convent and, in particular, in the chapel above the altar.

It was during this week that I also discovered a power within the Eucharist I had not touched into before. I paid more attention than usual to the words of the Liturgy and reflected on the meaning of the bread and wine as the body and blood of Christ. Within the Church of England, the bread and wine were symbolic, mere representations, but in the Catholic Church, the bread and wine actually became the body and blood of Christ. *Yuck,* I used to think. *How can the Church advocate feasting on human flesh and blood like a cannibal?*

But as I pondered these options and partook of the Eucharist on a daily basis, I noticed something changing. When I ate the bread, nothing much happened, but after drinking the wine as well, an inner fire would come up from either my heart or the depths of my belly, spreading throughout my body and mind and bringing a sense of peace and loving intimacy with Jesus. *Hmmmm.*

This was a taste of the overwhelming experience I'd had in the dream, a reminder. Occasionally I'd dismiss it as the effects of alcohol on a sensitive system, but surely not after one watered-down sip? When I went into the feeling, exploring it with awareness, it seemed that both the Anglican and Catholic traditions pointed to the Truth: As symbols, the bread and wine were ways to enter the mystery of who Jesus was and is. From within that mystery, where merging with Jesus happened and generated the experience of being one with Him, it seemed entirely possible that the transfiguration of the bread and wine into His body and blood had indeed taken place. It wasn't disgusting at all. Such was the purity of His body and blood they had become elixirs, transformative agents in their own right, brought about through an inner alchemy intrinsic to the consciousness of Jesus.

And so the silence deepened.

As the days passed, the chattering mind I was experiencing slowed down and quietened. Or so it appeared to the one observing. But who was the one observing? I hadn't yet learnt to ask that question but later, it would prove invaluable in the search for, and understanding of, the nature of the Self.

Instead, my experience was of a quality of silence that felt like being at the bottom of the sea. There was a heaviness, a fullness, about it. It seemed to engulf everything, pulling me inwards and away from superficial activities or words. The desire to speak receded, and I lost interest in any kind of conversation with fellow retreatants beyond necessities. But there was no sense of isolation or disconnection, and I didn't mind the presence of others; there was a sense of meeting and togetherness in the shared space. But there was no grasping, no effort, no social niceties, no concerns about what others might think, no needs of any kind.

What a relief! My job as a broadcaster meant a lot of talking. A lot of words, of engagement with people that required intense questioning, and heaven forbid there was ever any silence; "dead air" was the broadcaster's nightmare. Yet here I was, discovering how much life was being restored in the acres and hours of "dead air" within and around me.

Occasionally, a word or a sentence would float into my mind, and I would look at it. Was this useful? Did it need to be spoken? Was it worth interrupting the silence, emerging from this golden cocoon, to make ripples on the surface of the water with a few words? So often, it wasn't, and the words would float away like spectres into the dark.

The more I let go, the more important it seemed that speech, if it were to be proffered, carried within it the essence of this Noble Silence, and so transmitted something of that inherent fullness of beauty and love to whoever received the words.

Words became living entities, language revealed its power to create or destroy, and much in between. But those words that carried the essence of silence were sacred. They touched the soul and could open it to a remembrance of its core essence and where it came from. They could reach out across the abyss and grab your attention, drawing you back to the Source from where all life originates. These words were not just words; they were agents of the Divine!

"In the Beginning was the Word", the primordial sound emerging from a vast nothingness, the very beginning of the journey of pure energy into manifest form. The Ancients in the East call that sound *OM*. Was that the Word? Or was the Word already more formed than this resounding syllable implies?

As my week drew to a close, I had settled into the rhythm of monastic life and silence so comfortably I didn't want it to end. I never wanted to speak again. I could have lived in retreat like this forever.

I still believed that if I wanted anything enough, it could happen; that if I found something I liked, then that experience of liking would never change; that finding what I liked and getting really attached to that was the way to find lasting happiness. I had no real understanding of the nature of mind, and therefore, no idea that such thoughts and beliefs were completely at odds with the true spiritual path.

What I did realize was that there was a significant difference between being on retreat, left to my own devices and without responsibility, and being a member of the community, where responsibilities abounded and vows kept everyone and everything in order. It was not possible to stay more than a short period in retreat, lest enthusiasts like me get tempted perhaps to book in for a life of idle escapism.

But I didn't much like the look of life on the other side, either: all those very early starts, unattractive clothes, being told what to do, no break from the routine, total confinement, incessant readings from the Bible, and worse than school, no option to question its authority or deviate from the vow of obedience (or chastity, for that matter).

Fulfilled and content as I was in the convent, I realized that exchanging my worldly life with all its pitfalls and challenges for the life of a nun was probably "too soon". I was in my twenties and, despite the freedom I'd felt during my week, a lifelong commitment felt like an early grave, and I knew I couldn't do it.

My inner silence was shattered; thoughts came crashing in. An overwhelming sense of familiarity with life as a nun took hold, and it seemed as if memories from other lives came flooding in: quiet, peaceful lives; lives of unhappy cloistering against my will; lives of persecution; lives of aching for a "love" outside the monastery. No, I couldn't take this path.

I'd also tasted a few "forbidden fruits" and had a strong sense that there was the possibility of as genuine a spiritual path in a sexual relationship as there was in a life of celibacy. One was not better than the other. In fact, the cruelty of some nuns and the misery etched in certain faces convinced my young mind that giving up sex for the wrong reasons was a bad idea. I had no idea if this was the reason behind their alleged cruelty, but when I thought of how bad-tempered I could be when sexually frustrated, I assumed they might be the same. I wasn't familiar with the mental habit of "projection" and, like many people, saw much of the world through the eyes of my own experience.

Throughout the turbulence of this penultimate day, answers were coming thick and fast. I had discovered a way to connect deeply with the experience of my dream, with the love of Jesus, and I admired the nuns who'd stepped into this life, for better or worse. I was like them in some respects, but oh so different in others.

Those differences were sending me back into the world, to search elsewhere for a place to live out my vocation. I was hugely grateful for this week in the convent, and sad to leave. I left in an in-between state, neither fully in the world nor completely out of it. It was a confusing place to be—a place that Buddhists would refer to as a *bardo* and regard as an opportunity, a gap in the apparent solidity of experience that offered a glimpse into a much greater truth.

However, I just felt confused. I returned to my job and my home, and life carried on without any major interruptions or change externally. I thought things might settle, but they didn't. Like low grumblings of thunder in the background, I couldn't get away from what I had been shown and told in my dream, and I knew that there had been many people throughout history who had found themselves on a quest for Truth, for that "peace which passeth all understanding". I wasn't going to be let off that hook.

Chapter 2
Healing Hands

After the disappointment of not finding my answer in the life of a monastic, my thoughts turned to the only other formal expression of a Christian vocation I knew: the Church itself.

I had been both baptized and confirmed in the Church of England and, despite my love of the "bells and smells" of high ritual in the Catholic Church and indeed, its greater focus on Mary, Mother of Jesus, which felt balancing to me, I wasn't about to undergo a full conversion.

As a broadcaster for BBC Radio Oxford, I had recently started my own programme, one I'd been dreaming of for years and finally been given permission to do. It was called *My Life* and featured hour-long interviews with the great and the good of the county telling their life story with selected pieces of music to complement this. It was not unlike Radio 4's long-standing *Desert Island Discs* but with a touch of *In the Psychiatrist's Chair*, or so I liked to think. I'd trained in Psychology at university and was very interested in the deeper drives behind people's choices in life and how certain key events shaped their thinking, their beliefs, and who they were as people.

One of my guests had been The Rt. Rev. Richard Harries, then Bishop of Oxford. I'd enjoyed meeting him enormously and found his capacity to talk about spiritual matters very compelling. Here was someone whose life and work were both deeply informed by his faith and who'd found a way to be "in the world" whilst having his sights firmly focused on much that was not "of this world".

I wondered if he could help. If anyone could guide me through this discernment process in relation to the Church, I felt that he could. On receipt of my letter, he kindly agreed to see me, and I ventured over to his home office in North Oxford. I remember being somewhat intimidated by the library of religious books that filled the shelves and tabletops of Bishop Richard's comfortable room, but I noted with particular interest his most recent publication, *Art and the Beauty of God* (Mowbray, 2000).

We chatted over a very English cup of tea, and whilst I couldn't pretend this was a cosy cuppa with the local parish vicar, our conversation flowed easily and happily, with tables somewhat turned, as I was the one revealing thoughts and feelings I wouldn't readily share with many.

Things were going well, until the question: "Which church do you attend?"

Silence. Memories of my interview at Wadham College flooded in, followed by those of my job interview at Radio Oxford.

I recalled my acute embarrassment when asked by the German tutors at Wadham to show understanding of a poem they'd given me about Orpheus.[1]

"Do you know the name of Orpheus's wife?" they had asked.

I did not . . . despite the fact that it was written in the poem I had just read! I was too nervous to take much in and instead, stumbled and blurted out, "Well, it wasn't Apollo, because Apollo was a bloke."

Oh God, I couldn't believe these words had actually come out of my mouth. One of the tutors burst out laughing, and I turned bright pink, but then he kindly guided my agitated, blurred attention to another line later in the poem.

"Oh, Eur-ee-dike," said I.

"Eury-dee-see!" said he.

Fast-forward to the manager's office at Radio Oxford, where I was interviewed by a board of three managers and editors. I remember nothing of this interview beyond the ever-changing cloudscapes outside the window that captured my gaze as I struggled to answer questions about local politics and editorial policies. But I recalled that I *hadn't* been rejected; I'd got into Oxford and I'd got into the BBC. There was hope.

So I said: "I don't go to church."

Bishop Richard looked a little surprised, but skilfully moved the conversation to assist me in finding a Church I might feel an affinity with and start there. He ascertained that High Anglican might suit my Catholic leanings and suggested Mary Magdalene Church in central Oxford. The presiding priest was well respected and apparently gave good, intelligent sermons; frankincense was wafted liberally; and Sunday service was conducted as a Mass. I was enthusiastic and gratefully bounced out of the bishop's office to begin the next stage of my quest. Was I destined to become Rev. Howard once I'd got the hang of this Church thing?

The following Sunday, I made my way to the church and took my place in the congregation. I sang along with the hymns, listened to the sermon, took Holy Communion, and entered into the Liturgy with as much open-hearted curiosity and willing participation as I could muster. But it felt alien. I felt like a fraud, paying lip service to the words on the pages in front of me, singing along to hymns, whilst recalling the time I'd spent in an Evangelical church in London; all that happy guitar-playing and waving of arms in the air made me want to run for the hills. I was feeling something similar here. Although there was nothing Evangelical about this church, I felt imprisoned nonetheless and not an integral part of what was happening.

I came out of the Sunday service with a heavy heart. This was definitely not the way forward, and I was sad I no longer resonated with an institution that had informed so much of my childhood and early days of spiritual exploration. I felt unplugged, dislocated, at sea. I didn't belong anymore, and that was why I'd stopped going to church. It had happened so naturally, without any particular judgement or thought. I'd just stopped going; life had been taken over by other interests and responsibilities. Until I set foot back inside with a serious intention to ordain as a minister, it had never occurred to me that I had well and truly left the established Church.

It seemed that following this vocation was becoming a process of elimination: not that, not that, and not that either! As the obvious doors closed, so the burning quest intensified. I wasn't going to give up; I couldn't. Life was perfectly pleasant in many ways but deeply unsatisfying in others, and I knew that wouldn't change unless I was the one to make that change.

How often do we set off in search of an answer to a big question by travelling away from home, investigating new and unfamiliar worlds, stretching beyond comfort zones, in the belief that happiness lies somewhere entirely different? If I'm not happy here, then surely "there" I will be—in this new job, this new city, this new lifestyle. It couldn't possibly be the case that my answer, or at least the beginning of it, might be right under my nose, that I might already be living into it, just as the early 20th century German poet Rainer Maria Rilke had so wisely advised his young poet friend:

> Have patience with all that remains unsolved in your heart. Try to love the questions themselves, like locked rooms and like books written in a foreign language. Do not look for the answers. They cannot be given to you because you could not live them. It is a question of experiencing everything. At present you need to *live* the question. Perhaps you will gradually, without even noticing it, find yourself experiencing the answer, some distant day.[2]

In many ways, I'm still living the question 30 years later, but there have been periods when I've lived my way into answers, too. These answers sometimes lead to more questions or a refinement of the central question. Equally, though, they bring me closer to an understanding of how to make what seemed to be such a big journey from my everyday self to the true self that was revealed in my dream.

Years before the dream, I'd set out on a different journey; I was with a boyfriend who suffered regular bouts of debilitating back pain and was in the midst of one such episode whilst visiting me. I offered to give him a backrub and whilst doing so, took my hands off his back and just held them a few centimetres above his spine.

"Oh, what have you done?" he suddenly asked.

"Nothing," I replied.

He turned around and looked at me, somewhat shocked. "Well, the pain has gone. I felt something like an electric shock going up and down my spine and then the pain vanished."

I was equally shocked and had no idea how it had happened. I remember thinking, *I don't want to be a witch!* Then promptly pushed it to the back of my mind.

But it's not usually possible to push such things away forever, and it kept bothering me. I look back and wonder why I was so convinced it meant I might be a witch, as if this were a bad thing. I was strongly conditioned by the Church, which tended to view any power it couldn't explain, own, or control as that "of the Devil". Unconsciously, perhaps, I was aware of how history had condemned many women with healing gifts to death. But I also knew this "miracle healing" had offered real help, and surely that was something to take seriously in a positive way? I had forgotten that the Church had a strong tradition of healing as ministry, but even so, my own path was destined to move away from the Church, and challenges to deep and often unconscious conditioning were part of that.

Browsing the shelves in a bookshop one day, a book entitled *Healing Hands* by Allegra Taylor (Optima, 1992) caught my attention. Relief flooded my body as I flicked through the pages and recognized my own experience staring back as if from a mirror. A list of recommended organizations at the back of the book felt like signs, and I wrote down the address for the National Federation of Spiritual Healers.

It wasn't long before I was referred to a healer to apprentice myself with. In her early 80s, Joy had been a healer for much of her adult life. She was one of the kindest people I had ever met, and although I couldn't see colours around people, I was convinced she was surrounded by gold. She was a simple soul, who'd been happily married for over 40 years. She practised from her living room, where clients came to see her for hands-on healing sessions. She had a strong faith and often worked with Jesus or the Angels, but she never imposed this on anyone else. She offered unconditional love and directed this loving energy into a person's body and energy field.

I was taught more formally how to conduct a full healing session. With a client seated in a comfortable chair or on a stool, it was important to be able to reach their back without obstruction. Prayers to connect with the Divine began the session, whereupon healing energy was then requested for the client. There were certain recommended hand positions, moving around the body in sequence, both lightly touching the person and holding the hands a few centimetres away but still within the auric field. A healer might spend longer in some places if there was a specific problem in that area, or if the hands felt "stuck"—areas requiring healing would often pull it in, creating a kind of suction effect on the healer's hands, which would often be generating noticeable heat by this point. Generally, however, the healing energy was understood to have an intelligence of its own, which would work with the client's own intelligence (usually unconsciously) and be directed to where it was needed and could most usefully be applied in that moment.

I wasn't aware of a great deal of science that could explain the phenomenon of healing, at the time. I don't think there was much. There were stories and anecdotal evidence detailing its benefits. Some bordered on the miraculous; others were less dramatic, perhaps nothing more than a lift in mood. Furthermore, my own experience was enough to convince me, both as a giver or receiver of healing, that it made a tangible difference.

In the intervening years, there's been a good deal more research into the effects of "positive energy" on mind and body, and how it can significantly improve life expectancy, recovery from illness or surgery, and general wellbeing. It seems so obvious, but when we consider how dissociated so many of us have become from what's going on inside ourselves, and how much we turn to and rely on external solutions for our health and wellbeing, perhaps it isn't surprising that the power of healing is met with such scepticism.

As my apprenticeship continued, I was encouraged to begin practising on friends and family, and the feedback was universally positive. Everyone reported greater feelings of calm, peace, and a sense of connection and optimism. At this stage, no one presented with any serious medical condition, and any change perceived was only at the emotional or mental level, leaving much scope for the argument that healing was nothing more than a placebo effect; that is, people felt better simply because of the positive attention they were receiving. But, as I reasoned at the time, babies died or thrived depending on the amount of love they received. Surely our adult systems were not so very different, no matter how developed the rational aspect of the brain?

My confidence grew, and I began to receive the odd referral, working from home or going to a client's house (we called them "patients" in those days, but I now prefer to use the term "clients" as it's less pathologizing) in my own time outside broadcasting work.

Then, through a mutual friend, I met a lovely woman called Pat who'd just set up a complementary health clinic in nearby Wantage. We clicked immediately, recognizing in each other, kindred spirits and sharing a wish to facilitate health and healing for others. When I explained that I didn't charge for my healing, accepting donations only, she promptly offered me the use of a room in her clinic once a week at no cost.

And so I started to see clients on a Thursday evening; the physical space and professional context creating a new focus for the sessions and a healthy boundary around the work. I never found it draining—quite the opposite, in fact—but it wasn't always easy to set clear boundaries around sessions and that seemed to weaken the intensity of the healing energy.

One day, I got a phone call from an old friend. Could I see a friend of her mother's who'd just been given a terminal diagnosis after seven years of battling breast cancer and a fortnight to live? I didn't know what to say. This was a frighteningly advanced stage of an illness, and I hadn't worked with anyone with such a serious medical condition. What were her expectations? Could I help her? Was it appropriate? All these questions raced through my mind, but I wanted to help and had a strange feeling that Ann had been "sent" for a reason. There was something for us to do together. And so I said yes.

The woman who walked into the clinic a week later was clearly not well, but her spirits were bright and she was optimistic and determined.

"I want another year," she told me. "The doctors have said they can't do anymore, and there'll be no more chemo or treatment, but I'm not ready to go."

I tried not to reveal how apprehensive I was feeling. A weight of expectation landed on me but, as I always did in a healing session, I offered it up and asked God, Jesus, and the Angels to work through me to bring whatever healing or comfort possible to Ann.

I placed my hands on her head and began the session. As I worked around her body, I became more and more aware of how very sick her body was. It felt like a shell that was emptying out its contents of a human being. It was quite a shock. It felt too late, and this feeling was confirmed when I "saw" a silvery, shimmering human form with a cord rather like an umbilical cord attached to this body.

This was Ann's spirit. She was already leaving her body! I'd never felt or seen this before, but there it undeniably was, and the contrast between the health and vitality of her spirit and the very sick condition of her body was so great that I felt I now knew for certain that, whilst we may inhabit and bring life to a body, we are not our body; we are so much more than our physical existence.

My heart opened more than usual as I began to see what was happening, and the peace that filled the room was palpable. It was as if the Angels were coming so close, coming to take her home. I was very moved and somewhat overwhelmed by the whole experience. I didn't expect to see Ann again, but as she left the room looking relaxed and quite radiant, I was grateful she'd been given something that I prayed would help her.

The following week, Ann returned for her next appointment. I couldn't have been more surprised to see the transformation that appeared to have happened. She looked a good deal stronger and was quite cheerful, telling me that she felt "30 percent better". When I put my hands on her this time, she was fully there, right back inside her body. *Okay,* I thought. *This is not the end. Let's see what unfolds from here and keep going.*

For six months, Ann continued to come every week, feeling considerably better than when she'd been sent home to die. She was optimistic and found great comfort, support, and healing in the sessions, and I continued to be amazed and moved by her progress. Towards the end of the year, however, things began to change, and Ann's health started to decline. She found the clinic stairs difficult, and her breathing was more laboured. I think we both recognized that the nature of our sessions was going to change, and that it was time now to focus on "healing into dying" and having as good a death as possible. I offered to see her at home, and she gratefully accepted.

I was completely out of my depth, in my late 20s with very little exposure to serious illness or death, but I knew how much Ann needed our sessions. I was very fond of her, so I decided I didn't need to understand or know what to do; my role was to continue offering her healing and trust that this was helping in ways I couldn't direct, see, or know.

Over several months, although Ann's health slowly deteriorated, her spirit seemed to become lighter and lighter. She was withdrawing internally from her outward responsibilities and relationships, and turning her attention increasingly towards Christ and her inevitable departure. Then, one day, I received a call from her son to say she'd been admitted to a hospice. I immediately went to see her.

"Are you okay, Ann?" I asked. She knew what I meant.

"Yes," she said. "It's all fine. I'll be okay to pop off at the weekend."

What an inspirational woman she was. I knew she'd got a handle on her own dying, and I knew she'd been given exactly what she'd asked for: another year. I didn't doubt that she was going to be okay and that the timing was perfect.

Ann died a few days later, at the weekend, sitting up in bed, placing a bet on her favourite horse race, The Grand National.

Chapter 3
Death

It was during my year with Ann that I had been exploring how to answer my growing sense of a calling. I never considered that there might be a link between these two experiences. When Ann died, I was caught between joy at her extraordinary mastery over death and sadness that she had gone. I sat with these contradictions and the feelings of loss at the same time as I sat with the realization that I had probably exhausted the conventional vocational routes and didn't know how to move forward.

As Ann's death became inevitable, I began to notice how often people would glaze over when the subject of dying came into the conversation. Instead of support, I started to experience a kind of isolation, which confused and distressed me at first, until I realized that the reason was probably fear. People didn't know what to say, and they didn't really want to get involved. I was pretty scared myself at the prospect of Ann's death and how it would be, but I hadn't anticipated a generalized fear about the subject amongst folk who weren't personally touched by what was happening.

As I reflected further, it occurred to me that we weren't very good at facing or coping with death in our British culture. In the past, we lived alongside death: mortality was much higher across the age spectrum and families had no choice but to look after dying and deceased relatives. But in our modern culture, death tended to be hidden away, and everything in our medical, legal, and political system focused on keeping people alive, for as long as possible, as if death were some great failing or insult to our human rights.

What I'd just experienced, however, was a peaceful, even beautiful death that was entirely natural and affirming of a degree of personal power and choice about how it unfolded. It may have been that Ann's faith and the healing had played a significant part in her exceeding medical expectations and in her coming to terms with dying in ways that gave her freedom in its midst, but either way, I noticed in myself a growing urge to "do something" to help people face death—their own or that of someone close.

I also realized that the many changes and losses that come with death come with a great many other life events. Any ending that impacts us emotionally and/or physically can be like a death: a relationship breakup, job loss, sudden disability, and on a bigger scale, natural disasters, wars, and enforced exile. Even seemingly positive life events involving big change can be accompanied by a sense of something ending. Change is happening to us all the time, and the bigger and more unexpected it is, the less we are prepared and the more we suffer.

Reflecting on all this, an idea slowly dawned on me. I would write a book—a book of interviews with a wide range of people who'd all experienced death in ways that had been life-changing and could talk openly and honestly about what they'd been through. In so doing, I hoped to bring death out from under the carpet a little more and enable others to find a sense of belonging and support at a time when it was easy to feel alone and afraid.

It was with this idea that I found my way forward.

The book fell into place as if divinely orchestrated. Within a week of committing to the idea, I had an editor (through a writer friend), a publishing contract, and a modest advance. I also had my first interviewees: Dame Cicely Saunders, founder of the hospice movement, and a family who'd lost their son to leukaemia in his 20s.

Others I found were an Oxford couple whose determination to face their death well ahead of the event resulted in their making their own coffins and storing them in the garden shed, a woman whose partner had Alzheimer's and was enduring the difficult deterioration of her partner's mental acuity and personality long before her physical death, and a prisoner serving life for the murder of his girlfriend.

I was fortunate to meet Sir Isaiah Berlin and take note of his philosophical approach to his own death. I spoke to psychiatrist Dr. Anthony Storr, whose near-death experience after a severe asthma attack radically altered his perspective on life, and I met two Buddhist teachers, whose understanding of death and dying surpassed anything I'd encountered. Most extraordinary perhaps was the story of Dadi Janki, the European head of the Brahma Kumaris World Spiritual University. Like Lazarus, she had returned to life after two episodes of clinical death! They were all diverse individuals, each sharing the same ultimate fate as every single human being on this planet.

Less than a year later, in 1996, *Death: Breaking the Taboo* was published by Arthur James, Ltd. Writing the book was a privilege and a joy. The courage, wisdom, and compassion of all those I interviewed came through their stories and I hoped offered a reassuring hand in the dark to anyone who needed that.

Whilst I was doing my research for this book, I'd discovered Sogyal Rinpoche's now classic book, *The Tibetan Book of Living and Dying* (HarperCollins, 1994). This book turned out to be pivotal in many ways.

Sogyal Rinpoche had woven together his knowledge of traditional Tibetan Buddhist teachings about death and dying (most notably from *The Tibetan Book of the Dead)* and his understanding and experience of the Western mind and culture. It was a brilliant idea and a great success when it was first published in 1992.

Reading this book, however, was not just a useful exercise, offering an interesting perspective; it made a profound impression on me and, over and over, I would get this strange sense of being reunited with teachings I already knew, accompanied by a feeling of extraordinary familiarity. It was as if the book was unlocking a "knowing" that had been there a very long time. This was confusing, because I hadn't encountered Tibetan Buddhism before picking up this book, and no one in my family or circle of friends had had anything to do with it, either. Where was this feeling coming from, and why did I keep hearing the words in my head *This is what I've been looking for*, spoken like an echo from a cave deep in my heart?

During my radio years, I'd befriended the entomologist George McGavin, who worked at Oxford University at the time. He was a Scot with a terrific sense of humour and an enthusiasm for insects, which baffled and intrigued me in equal measure. I shared my book project with him as well as the connection I felt with the Tibetan teachings, and he immediately suggested that I should go to Samye Ling, a Tibetan Buddhist monastery in Scotland. I'd never heard of it, but I thanked him and decided to look it up.

I was in the habit of going on a one-week retreat every autumn, and after the publication of my book in July, a visit to Samye Ling seemed like the natural next step, so I booked a room for a week at the monastery in October and got on with my life.

I was no longer working in broadcasting and instead, had taken a job at the Prison Phoenix Trust in Oxford, a charity that supports the wellbeing of prisoners through literature, classes, and correspondence focusing on yoga and meditation. I knew a little about meditation, having been introduced to it through the World Community for Christian Meditation movement set up by John Main and led by Fr. Lawrence Freeman, a Benedictine monk. It was through another significant friendship—with biographer Shirley du Boulay—that I'd found my way to the cushion, and to the calming of the chattering mind that meditation could foster.

October came, and I made the long drive from my home in Woodstock to Samye Ling just over the border into Dumfries and Galloway. The changing scenery, particularly north of Manchester, reinforced the impression I had of travelling to another country. Once the M6 was carving its way through the Lake District, layers and layers of unknown tension fell away, as my soul expanded into the beauty of the hills and valleys that passed all too quickly with the speedy progress of the car on the motorway. Here, beyond industrialized middle England and the overcrowded South, there was SPACE, room to breathe. Nature still took precedence over people, and I was struck by how happy and free I began to feel.

In all spiritual traditions, there is an emphasis on the importance of "leaving home" when it comes to finding our true self. I recognized that this was another stage of leaving home, and this filled me with both excitement and sadness. I remembered all I'd learnt and discovered whilst writing the book about death, endings, and change and found some solace in knowing that I was on track with the familiar feelings surrounding big changes: New beginnings were on offer, as much as endings were also playing in the waves of my heart and mind.

Driving towards Eskdalemuir, the roads became more and more empty, and the natural landscape opened into a lowland range of hills clad in heather and Douglas fir trees. There was a silence and a quality of light that hinted at a sun just a little further away than usual. Logging was everywhere, and it saddened me to see the harvested hills as bare as a wasteland. I was reminded of the many brutal ways we humans use and exploit nature and how little respect is offered to the land in our greed and consumption.

Rounding a corner, I spotted colourful prayer flags flapping in the breeze and a series of buildings set up on the hillside on the left. I passed a village hall, and Samye Ling on the right came into clear view.

The entrance was unremarkable, the road bumpy and full of puddles (I was later to learn that Eskdalemuir was one of the wettest places in the British Isles!). There was an old stone house in the middle of the land, much older than the modern building that formed the guest house and the many wooden huts and cabins that made up the accommodation for the monastic and lay community.

I parked my car and made my way across the garden to reception, where I confirmed my booking and was given a key to my room. *I've come a long way to spend a week in a rainy, muddy boot camp,* I thought. *Better find out what this is all about and make the most of it.*

I went for a wander and soon found myself walking up the steps to the temple. Traditionally Tibetan, it was rectangular and had several storeys diminishing in size as they went up, culminating in a golden roof with upturned corners. Red brick was decorated with bright colours between storeys, and the huge wooden doors boldly displayed giant golden hinges, knobs, and other details.

But nothing could have prepared me for the interior. I gasped as I walked in, overwhelmed by the shimmer of gold and the vivid colours wherever I looked. There were great big upright gongs in wooden frames, lines of maroon meditation cushions, *thangka* paintings hanging from the walls, two large whirling prayer wheels, cloth-bound elongated texts piled behind huge glass-fronted cabinets, and hundreds of small golden Buddha statues surrounding an enormous central Buddha sitting serenely at the far end of the shrine room. It was impressive! It was very still, yet there was a wakeful, dynamic quality to the stillness. I'd had a long journey, but walking into the temple, I felt energized by it all, as much as I felt quietened and calmed.

I didn't know what to do. This was a foreign environment in many ways, and I had the impression that social convention wasn't going to get me very far. I didn't know very much about Tibetan Buddhism, and I was still rooted in Christian theology and orientation. It was confusing to be following a calling to "get back to Jesus" and find myself in a place as far removed from Christianity as was imaginable.

What I did notice, however, was how many young people around my own age were monks and nuns. They were mostly Westerners with shaved heads and wearing traditional maroon robes and wooden prayer beads around their necks or wrists. Some were friendly, others were not; many had tattoos and spoke with regional dialects. In this world, where appearances really didn't matter and vanity was actively discouraged, I became self-conscious. With my middle-class background, very English accent, make-up, and rather smart appearance, I felt like a fish out of water.

As the week went on, Samye Ling began to feel like a hall of mirrors, and I grew more and more uncomfortable in my own skin. But I'd also begun to wonder if this really *was* my skin. Peering out from behind this facade was someone else, and I felt exposed, as a clear distinction between the "social" and the "private" me became apparent. It was the private, more genuine person who seemed more interesting to the community, and this was perplexing, too.

At first, I couldn't hold a conversation for any length of time, as the bewildering inner see-sawing between my conditioned self and natural self muddled my thoughts and speech. I stopped wearing make-up, fearing looks of horror and anticipating rejection as I ventured out in public (I'd no idea I was so insecure!). No one noticed. I sat with others in the temple in formal meditation or prayer sessions (known as *pujas*), in the dining room at lunch, and in the cafe and the sitting room. I observed, watched, listened, occasionally contributed, and slowly the feelings of isolation, difference, and separation softened. I liked these people. They were funny and earthy, refreshingly "real", from all walks of life, clearly quite troubled in many cases, or having had difficulties in life.

There was one monk in particular, with a broad Scottish accent, who went out of his way to make me feel welcome. He seemed quite intense, moving and speaking very fast, but he was kind. In fact, everyone was kind, and I was struck by that. It wasn't a kindness designed to just make you feel better about yourself; rather, it was a kindness that freed you from having to hold yourself together in ways that were imprisoning or inauthentic. If you were suffering inside, that was welcomed and regarded as a positive thing to acknowledge—after all, the Buddha's teaching directly addressed suffering, and there was no true entering the Eightfold Buddhist path without fully seeing the First Noble Truth: *The Truth of Suffering.*

As I relaxed into Samye Ling more and more, so I relaxed into myself, or was it the other way round? I noticed that I was happy. By the time the week was over, I didn't really want to leave, and yet I had a life to return to and was looking forward to going back. I said goodbye to my new friends, and the nice young monk came to see me off in the car park. He looked wistful as I drove away, and I was glad we'd exchanged addresses. Bumping over the muddy potholes, I knew that I'd found something special at Samye Ling, and made a mental note to thank George, as I turned out of the driveway and began the long journey back south.

Chapter 4

Trouble in the Monastery

I was home and returned to life as normal. Except that it wasn't normal. I couldn't settle back into my routines, and apathy and indifference infused activities that once would have brought me joy. My relationship was in trouble, and my work contract was coming to an end. I had a mortgage to pay, the prospect of which felt like clambering back onto a hamster wheel and tying myself to a life that no longer had much meaning.

I wondered what my Scottish friend would make of this, and if he'd had a similar experience before his decision to leave the city and become a monk.

We exchanged letters and, although his circumstances had been very different to mine, he'd reached a kind of disillusionment with his life that seemed similar to my own, at least in part. The more I thought about it, the more I felt stuck in a life going nowhere in particular; a life that had allowed me to taste much of what many people aspire to but that ultimately hadn't brought me lasting happiness or peace of mind.

I began to look forward to his letters, written with an openness of heart and an honesty that was so refreshing. I'd spent years in environments where the mind and mental faculties took precedence, where feelings were swept under carpets, and I'd rebelled against the coldness and disconnection that this oh-so-British habit led to. My soul was thirsty for a different way of being.

Almost imperceptibly, sensing I may have met a kindred spirit, a soul mate of sorts, my feelings grew and I realized that I was in danger of falling for my monk friend. I tried to suppress these feelings, but as his letters hinted at a shared affection, I started to allow myself to feel them. I knew that he was a monk, and nothing could happen between us, but at the same time I knew that love was a powerful force, sometimes inconvenient but to be respected and ultimately trusted.

If I'd known then what I know now, this book might never have been written. But the wisdom of hindsight is no good when you're busy gaining that wisdom the hard way! I'd always been a romantic, with a heart full of love and the longing to love and be loved. At age 30, I'd had a number of heartbreaks already, and relationships were my nemesis more often than the source of what I'd been hoping for. Well-meaning friends and family frequently consoled me with suggestions that I needed to look elsewhere for an appropriate partner, and suddenly their advice appeared to make sense. Of course! I needed a spiritual partner, someone with whom I could share these interests and "the journey".

Love was pure. Love was the point of any spiritual path. Maybe love was ultimately more real and closer to God than even being a monk or a nun. Sometimes the monastic life was just running away, I told myself. Or it might come to a natural end, having served its purpose, in much the same way as many marriages or other life commitments come to an end.

My mind went round and round, coming up with all manner of reasons why this might be happening and why it was okay—or at least justifiable—to keep open.

But beyond (or integral to) the attraction of the man was the attraction of Buddhism itself. I knew that I'd found something I really wanted to explore, if not fully immerse myself in. As my life in

Oxfordshire paled into insignificance, so the prospect of a new life up in Scotland at the monastery filled in all the gaps.

* * *

But there was a problem: I owned a house. To leave it for any length of time, without an income to pay the mortgage, was not an option. Renting it out would solve that problem, but wouldn't give me enough money to pay for my new life. I didn't know what to do.

The impasse continued for some time, my frustration mounting. Then one day, I decided to take a leaf out of the Buddha's own book and sit beneath my apple tree, as the Buddha had once sat beneath the bodhi tree, until I got an answer. I wouldn't move until an answer came, clear and unmistakable.

So I settled myself down, ready to endure night and day there if that's what it took. Time passed. My mind chattered on automatic, occasionally falling silent, occasionally more reflective or just floating off. Then suddenly, as clear as if someone was standing beside me, I heard the words, like an instruction: *Sell your house.*

Time stopped. Six hours had passed. There was no mistaking the message, but my mind panicked. There was no safety in this! Not only in the act itself, if I followed through, but in the sharp precision of the unembellished instruction—there were no soothing securities or reassurances. I'd got what I asked for, but I didn't like it one bit.

Well, I thought, if this was "God talking", I needed to ask for more signs. Only a fool would put their house on the market on the strength of three words heard, perhaps imagined, under an apple tree. I made a deal with God and with myself that if I got another clear message with the same instruction, I would do it.

That night, I slept soundly but woke earlier than usual. Without thinking, I turned over to put the radio on. The mellifluous tones of *Prayer for the Day* on Radio 4 greeted me. And there it was: the story of the Israelites being sent out into the wilderness, after Pharaoh finally released them from slavery in Egypt with nothing but makeshift homes and rooftops of leaves.

I lay there stunned. If ever there were a prophetic instruction, there it was. I took the fact that I'd randomly turned on the radio at a time I rarely did, only to hear this passage from the Bible, as a clear sign that I too was meant to head out into the unknown and give up the comfort and security of my bricks-and-mortar home.

Of course, most people thought I was mad and did their very best to dissuade me from selling up and moving on without any clear landing in place. I understood and agreed with all the arguments, but, every time I gave up my "irresponsible idea", I sank back into the doldrums and found no joy or reason to carry on. The lights just went out. So, quietly, without telling anyone, I made tentative enquiries with a local estate agent, who confirmed a value of the house in excess of what I'd paid for it—just enough to give me a small sum with which to head out into the "wilderness".

There was no stopping me after that. The house had served its purpose beautifully, and I was ready to let it go. I thought fondly of the time we'd shared, the work I'd done to improve it, and the much greater potential it had for further improvement. It had looked after me for nearly three years, and I was determined to find the right people to take it on—people who would benefit from what it had to offer, would look after it, and whose values were aligned with my own. In that way, I could leave in peace. I wasn't so bothered about who offered the best price; I would choose the people I felt the house would enjoy and who would love the house.

Within a week of it being on the market, several offers were made on the house. A bit shocked, I hadn't expected such a difficult decision to be resolved so quickly and easily as soon as I'd made it! The serious offers were all good, but there was one particular family I wanted to sell the house to—they were expecting their second child: the mother a nurse, the father a legal aid lawyer. I accepted their offer, and the sale went ahead, teetering only briefly as the family struggled to confirm a mortgage but on track in every other respect.

* * *

Within two months, it was gone, and I'd moved out. My family was horrified. I felt liberated. In the intervening weeks since the broadcast that sealed my fate and my actual departure, I'd settled on the idea of going up to Samye Ling for a period. I could stay in the Guest House and see how it went. I didn't want to tie myself down to any commitments anywhere at this point and, although I'd filled in and sent off the forms to become a resident volunteer, I wasn't seriously considering this role and didn't wait for a reply. The freedom of being a paying guest felt more true to the spirit of stepping into the Unknown.

I'd let my Scottish friend Yangdak know my plans and had wondered if they were making him a bit nervous, as his letters had become more guarded, I felt. I didn't want him to feel under any pressure, or indeed responsible for my actions in any way, and hoped I'd been able to reassure him that this decision was in keeping with a sense of vocation sparked long before I had encountered Samye Ling or met him. True, it was hard to tease apart my interest in Buddhism from my interest in him, especially as he embodied the Buddhist path for me, in his monastic robes, but I felt clear in my conscience and genuine in my motivation.

Driving back up the M6, I felt excited. This was a real adventure, and I had enough independent means not to feel too vulnerable. If I didn't like it, I could leave. I wasn't really planning to stay, anyway; just long enough to find my new feet, and my wings, and then, who knows what, who knows where? The world was my oyster. Such thoughts accompanied me on the long drive north.

I'd met the abbot of Samye Ling at an event quite recently. By coincidence he'd been in Oxfordshire, and I'd gone along to listen to him and meet him. Brimming with enthusiasm and self-confidence, I'd tried to talk to him over lunch, but he hadn't been very receptive.

I ventured to share my intentions about coming to Samye Ling, and he simply said "Have you been before?" in a tone indicating that I might be unpleasantly surprised by what I found there. "Yes," I answered, "just the once last year, and I loved it."

I thought nothing more of this, though I had been a little disappointed by his response. I wondered if it was a typically Buddhist response, cool and unattached, or if he'd taken a dislike to me for some reason. Well, it didn't matter, I reasoned. I could do my own thing and not have to have much to do with him. I forgot about him and continued with my plans.

Those plans had come to fruition now, and I was fast approaching the village of Eskdalemuir and, soon afterwards, the entrance to the monastery. The potholes were just as bad, and I took the road slowly enough to preserve my suspension and steady my excited nerves. To my surprise, the first person I saw, working in the vegetable garden on my right, was Lama Yeshe, the abbot. Cheerfully, I waved. He seemed none too pleased to see me, looking quite sternly in my direction before carrying on with whatever he was doing. Inwardly, I wobbled but shook it off quickly. I'd nothing to hide, nothing to worry about. What *was* his problem, I wondered?

I picked up the key to my room from reception and settled myself in, happy to be there and looking forward to seeing Yangdak. I hadn't mentioned any arrival date, but imagined I'd find him working in the café. This was his job, and he was a dab-hand at creating beautiful spaces. The greasy spoon "kaff", with its white plastic chairs and oily fry-ups, was undergoing major change, transforming into elegant Tibetan tea rooms that managed to combine the traditional colours and decor of a Tibetan space with the cosy comfort of a Scottish living room.

I wandered over, trying to appear cool and nonchalant. There he was, zipping about as if in a great hurry, serving customers whilst washing dishes and watching over the soup bubbling on the cooker. He caught sight of me and greeted me with warmth; perhaps more "professionally" than I'd expected, but nevertheless he seemed pleased to see me.

I ordered a coffee and took it to a table, settling down as best I could in my new temporary home. I'd given so much up to be where I was, but it had all been voluntary and felt like a natural next step and consequence of the intense searching, researching, reading, and writing I'd been involved in. But still, I had truly left home and pulled up all my roots, incurring the wrath and the concern of members of my family, and my position was hardly secure. *One moment at a time, just one step at a time. Don't push yourself, and don't rush into anything too soon*, I said to myself soothingly.

I felt more at ease around the café, with its more worldly ambience and my friend's presence, than around the rest of the monastery and decided this was a good spot to get used to everything. It was all so new and unfamiliar, and I hadn't a clue about how to live in such a place. I was just going to have to work it out as I went along. I'd also brought my tent, anticipating a real stint of living without a proper roof (I'd taken the Exodus story to heart) and feeling it was always good to have a backup plan and your own home, of sorts, if desperate, in tow. It was summer, and the fact camping could be fun was a bonus.

One afternoon, soon after my arrival, I was sitting outside the café when a senior monk came to sit at my table. A bit surprised, I opened conversation and received a similarly cool response as the one from the abbot.

He then turned to me, clearly a little nervous, and said: "I have a message from Lama Yeshe. He says he wants you to examine your motivation for being here, and if it has anything to do with Yangdak, he wants you to leave."

My eyes widened, my jaw dropped. I was shocked and stunned and stared at the senior monk in utter disbelief. My mind started to spin. I felt as if I'd been accused of a terrible crime, found guilty, and cast out like an "unclean woman", all in one fell swoop.

I was devastated, understanding in a split second why I'd been receiving such a cold reception from the abbot, but equally, feeling strung up like a witch without a fair trial and that I had to defend myself. But I also had to look at my motivation for being there and be honest with myself.

I felt terrible. I'd come with an open heart and positive intentions, following the trail that I was sure would lead me to the experience of being One with Christ, even if that meant dying to my old self, my old life. I'd stepped out in faith, in the blind assurance that everything would be okay. I'd found Samye Ling, a community and monastery where I felt I could fit in and belong. I'd even found a soulmate who perhaps might accompany me on this path more closely than I'd imagined any spiritual friend might. How could this be happening? I was bewildered and frightened. Could this abbot see something in or about me that I couldn't see myself? Or was he just imagining the worst, based on his own fears and wrong, or at least incomplete, assumptions?

Two days later, a letter arrived in the post. It had been forwarded from my home address in Woodstock. It was the reply from Samye Ling in response to my application to come and live there as a volunteer. I opened it and once more felt my world crumble and collapse as I read in print the words spoken to me outside the café. It was from the same senior monk, telling me in no uncertain terms that I was not welcome and kindly requesting me never to return to Samye Ling again.

The ferocity of the letter angered me as much as it upset me. How dare they? How dare they write me off like that, assuming my only motivation was to be with my monk friend, ignorant of all the events and the huge journey that had preceded this decision to come up to Samye Ling. But no wonder the abbot hadn't looked too thrilled to see me driving in! He must have thought I'd disregarded this decision to refuse my application, and come anyway.

Shaking with fear and anger, with the letter in hand, I marched to reception and asked if I might speak to Lama Yeshe. Phone calls were made. and all the while my heart was in my mouth and I just wanted the ground to open up beneath me and swallow me whole.

"He'll see you now," I was told.

Oh God, I thought. *Here we go. Nothing to lose now.*

Walking into the abbot's office, I noticed thick, brightly coloured carpets and wall hangings everywhere, photographs of various important people, the senior nun working at her desk at the back of the room. and Lame Yeshe sitting, relaxed and composed, in one of the high-backed brocade armchairs. I held out the letter:

"I gather you don't want me here," I uttered, fighting back tears whilst trying to sound indignant and innocent.

"No, I don't," he said.

At this point, I felt as if I was about to lose consciousness but noticed a huge fire running through my whole body. I was fixed to the spot and unable to move. I continued to explain, as best I could, that I hadn't received the letter in time not to come, and that my reasons for being there were far beyond my friendship with the monk in the café. I was still feeling the strange fire blazing within, and I could see that the abbot was aware of it, too.

He seemed to relax, looked at me with a little more curiosity, and said: "This is obviously karma. You are meant to be here. Okay, you can stay."

The fire dissolved, and I stood there shaking. I could stay! I was overjoyed to hear these words but still felt shock and fear. I left the room uttering grateful thanks and reassurances about my motivation to be there—vividly aware that there was no hanging about at Samye Ling on my own terms without having to interact with the scary abbot.

With the understanding I have now, I might have recognized and valued the extreme mental states I was subjected to as wonderful opportunities to both observe my mind and its habitual tendencies, as well as peer into the gap created every time shock interrupted thinking. I might have seen that the reactions I was having were coming from strong attachment to the "self" I believed myself to be and needed to protect. I might have seen that in rare moments when the thinking, whirring mind suddenly stopped, something else was present; it wasn't just "nothing".

But I had neither the understanding nor the tools to examine my experience in such depth, and I was simply tossed around on the stormy waves of my emotions and reactive thinking. I might also have realized that the abbot was trying to both protect me and his monks, to subvert any bad karma that might have resulted from interfering with the sanctity of the monastic robes. But I didn't see any of this at the time.

* * *

Untethered from my old life and not yet settled in a new one, I was aware of how vulnerable and insecure I could feel. I didn't have the same identity to fall back on, though I kept the narrative of my former life going for quite some time. How else could I describe who I was? How could I bridge the gap between strangers without talking about what I'd done?

I found that the book on death I had written, which after all was a major catalyst for my being there, became a point of entry into this new world. Buddhists are big on death and impermanence, and I'd found a way to join the club. I was also experiencing some of the aspects of death I'd been reading about and listening to from the stories of others.

Two or three weeks after my arrival at Samye Ling, I felt as if a part of me had begun to die. I experienced this as a kind of wistfulness, alongside a replaying of memories of my old life—people, places, events—that were superimposed onto the trees and buildings and moment-to-moment reality of the present situation, creating a kind of dreamlike existence. I was neither here nor there, floating between the past and the present, losing bearings, old anchor points and frames of reference. It was disorientating and uncomfortable, but every so often, I'd get a sudden feeling of strength or clarity, and I'd think, *Hey, this is more "me". This is more like it,* before losing it again in another swirl of emotion or thought.

In Buddhism, a lot of emphasis is placed on this intermediate state of being "in-between". I'd heard of the *bardo* and had noticed that the alternative name for *The Tibetan Book of the Dead* was the *Bardo Thodol.* So I knew I was in some kind of bardo state, and that this was natural and apparently positive. I thought: *Well, I'm in the right place to learn how to handle this. This is why I'm here. Perhaps I'd better shift my focus from the café to the temple.*

I also thought this would help with the strong feelings I was beginning to have towards my monk friend. Being asked to examine my motivation for being at Samye Ling, to see if it had anything to do with him, had brought this friendship into the foreground. The feelings that had been quietly growing over the months, well, I was perfectly aware of them, but hadn't anticipated any trouble because of them, either for myself or others.

But I'd realized that they were causing trouble, especially for others, and I felt self-conscious and somewhat guilty about this. I also became more confused as my friend clearly felt something similar and was struggling with his position as a monk with feelings and attraction towards a woman. I began to see why the abbot had feared my presence in the monastery might be a threat, and I determined to turn my mind to the Dharma and learning, in the hope of settling everything down. I was embarrassed about the trouble I had inadvertently caused.

Chapter 5
Gurus and Teachers

There was a rhythm to the day at Samye Ling, with prayers beginning early in the morning and ending in the evening. I rarely made it to the Tara prayers, which began at 6am, but would attend 8am meditation and sit for an hour, watching and feeling my mind and body, which were "on the go" more often than they were steady and calm.

I noticed that whenever the abbot was leading meditation, my anxiety would increase and sometimes border on panic, the impulse to get up and leave, run away, fighting with the discipline of staying put and weathering the inner storm.

Sometimes I wanted to burst into tears, as grief and sadness welled up from behind the fear. But these waves and storms would always pass, and whenever they did, my mind would settle right into the meditation and I learnt that these "obstacles" could actually be helpful. There seemed to be a direct relationship between the intensity of the mental anguish and the depth of the calm, steady presence of awareness once it had abated. I also realized that sitting in meditation with the abbot, a meditation master of high repute, was a great support. It might have brought issues to the surface, but it also empowered the ability to face and transform them—or at least let them be, after which they would mostly sort themselves out.

I had been meditating on and off for a couple of years, and it was more natural to attend the meditation sessions than the *pujas*, the daily prayers. These were all in Tibetan, of which I didn't speak a word, and were accompanied by instruments that were often harsh and quite loud. My first experience of the early afternoon Mahakala prayers was a definite shock, the huge gongs resounding alongside the clashing and crashing of cymbals was almost frightening.

Who's frightened? I would ask myself. This question always shifted my mind from fear to curiosity, opening a gap that allowed me to stay there and just watch, listen, notice that the sounds weren't actually hitting me, but they were shaking something loose.

As I relaxed into the experience, invariably I'd feel my mind expanding, becoming more spacious, my nervous system calming down. The fact I didn't understand the words wasn't a problem; not being distracted by words and their meaning was a blessing. My intellect, always wanting to understand and control everything, couldn't play in this arena. This gave other aspects of mind—insight and simple awareness—much greater freedom.

As the weeks passed, I began to understand what was happening whenever I sat in pujas or meditation in the temple. I'd been reading and studying the Buddhist view on the nature of suffering and its causes and how we could interrupt and eventually end this suffering. These preliminary teachings are referred to as The Four Noble Truths and represent the first cycle of teaching the Buddha gave after his enlightenment under the bodhi tree in Bodh Gaya, India.

Put simply, human beings have highly developed egos that lead us to see ourselves as separate entities operating in a world of other separate entities. This belief causes a lot of problems, as we move towards and desire pleasure and run away from and resist pain. All the familiar emotions of craving, longing, fear, anger, jealousy, and sadness, arise in response to this fundamental orientation, causing us to think, speak, and act in ways that are often unwise and cause suffering to ourselves and others. This way of being is so habitual, so unconscious for the most part, that we don't usually question it unless and until we become really fed up with the suffering and want to find a way out. Or perhaps we have an awakening experience, where we realize that there is far more to who we are than this ordinary human cycle of ups and downs might suggest.

The solution, so simple and yet so incredibly difficult, is to loosen the grip of the ego and our identity and liberate the mind into its true nature. That nature, our inherent Buddha nature, is beyond anything words can describe or the intellect can perceive, but it's generally described as vast, open, and clear, like a giant mirror that reflects anything and everything without judgement or interference. It has no characteristics, yet the qualities of compassion, love, joy, wisdom, and peace are spontaneously present, pure and dynamically alive.

The methods of Tibetan Buddhism I was being exposed to struck me as brilliant. They shook the mind free from its imprisonment within a narrow, limited understanding of itself through all kinds of "skilful means"; mostly, through quieting the agitated, everyday mind, logically examining the nature of reality, offering alternative, more enlightened identities (through Tantric deity practices), and allowing the mind to relax and rest in "open awareness".

My growing understanding and visceral experience of the impact of the practices soon convinced me that I'd found what I'd been looking for. I felt like I'd come home and reconnected with something that had always been inside me. As the initial sense of cultural alienation wore off, I began to have the opposite feeling: that I belonged in this Tibetan Buddhist world and that, whilst I didn't speak Tibetan, I was somehow familiar with the practices and teachings. Buddhists believe in reincarnation, and this would make sense of my experience, but I didn't want to confuse fantasy with reality or project familiarity with my true self onto another time or place. It was just wonderful to feel so much at home.

* * *

My obvious interest in the teachings reassured the abbot and the community, and trust grew. I made friends with a number of other people living there, and realized that I'd stepped into a big family of sorts. Brothers and sisters, many in robes, turned to each other with problems, jokes, stories and invariably a response would be offered that came from the Buddhist teachings and how they might be applied to all of our personal situations.

There are three touchstones at the heart of Buddhism, known as the "Three Jewels", upon which all spiritual progress depends. These are the Buddha himself, the Dharma (the body of Buddhist teaching), and the Sangha (the community of teachers or fellow students). I'd found my Sangha.

But this wasn't a pious, holier-than-thou community. Far from it! This was a community of very real people, many with challenging backgrounds, all with compassion and kindness as their focus, who were doing their best to face their own minds and transform their lives through transforming themselves. It was inspiring, touching, a relief. I loved it.

By now, I was volunteering in the Tea Rooms from time to time. I didn't have a formal position as a volunteer and was still living in the Guest House, but I wanted to help. I enjoyed Yangdak's company, and the Tea Rooms were the most normal interface with the general public and I felt comfortable and confident in that environment. Samye Ling received thousands of visitors every year, either attending courses, coming for a day out, or just passing by. It might have been stuck out in the middle of nowhere, 15 miles from the nearest town, but there was nothing isolating about being there.

I'd also discovered that, although Lama Yeshe was the abbot, running Samye Ling on a day-to-day basis, he wasn't the original founder. Samye Ling had been started by his older brother, Dr. Akong Tulku Rinpoche, and another young Tibetan teacher, Chögyam

Trungpa Rinpoche. All three men had endured and survived perilous journeys escaping Tibet, crossing the Himalayas into India, where they'd been welcomed but were living in exile.

Akong Rinpoche (*Rinpoche* is an honorific title in Tibetan Buddhism that means "Precious One", and *Tulku* means a "reincarnated teacher", who will often inherit responsibilities from a previous life) and Chögyam Trungpa were invited to Oxford, where Trungpa studied at the university whilst Akong Rinpoche earned money working as an orderly at the Radcliffe Infirmary. They had been offered a small Theravadin meditation centre, formerly an old hunting lodge, in Eskdalemuir to begin a Buddhist centre, and in 1967, they came to Scotland. With just a handful of students, the two Rinpoches began a new life.

The differences between them eventually led to a parting of ways, with Trungpa going to the United States in the early 1970s, where attitudes were more open to his experimental and occasionally shocking teaching methods and lifestyle choices. Akong Rinpoche took up the challenge of building a monastery in Scotland with virtually no money, very little English, and a workforce of volunteers.

Vin Harris, a long-time student of Akong Rinpoche first arrived around this time and remembers the early days with great affection. A university graduate, he laughs looking back on how it began for him:

> I started looking after the cows! I did that for over a year—so, from a literature degree to shovelling shit and feeding cows. It was a real spiritual apprenticeship, I guess. Rinpoche was living with us, right in the middle of it all, and it was a wonderful period.

Despite the challenges facing him, Rinpoche had a huge vision for Samye Ling. Believing at the time that he might never go back to Tibet, which had suffered so badly during the Cultural Revolution and was still being systematically destroyed, Samye Ling was intended to be something of a memorial to his homeland—architecturally, artistically, and culturally. It would also house sacred relics and traditional religious objects and be a thriving Dharma centre. He invited the best teachers and lineage holders from Tibet, most of whom were in exile in India, requesting that they teach the growing number of Western students gathering at Samye Ling and help to create a truly holy place.

It was with this in mind that plans for the main temple were drawn up. Sitting with Rinpoche in his house one day, watching a film, Vin recalls him turning to say, "I think we're going to build it ourselves." Vin found himself immediately volunteering help. He and other residents duly took themselves off to train in a number of building trades and crafts, returning to Samye Ling some months later ready to take on the huge task of building a traditional Tibetan temple from scratch.

> By 1978, the whole place had moved on and become this kind of craft village . . . there was a whole bunch of tin sheds, which were basically made out of scrap materials: woodwork shops, carving shops, art workshops, metal workshops. All of the main temple work was done in this "craft village".

Nearly 20 years later, when I first saw Samye Ling, a great deal of changes had taken place since the picture of those early days Vin painted. I knew very little and had never heard of or met Akong Rinpoche. He was away in Tibet when I first visited and was away again when I returned several months later. But his presence imbued every part of the place, and it became clear that this had been part of the magnetic force drawing me in.

My monk friend and I occasionally had to go out on shopping trips to buy things for the Tea Rooms. Unusually, for one such trip, we had to go to Edinburgh, a good 60 miles north. In my big old red Saab, it was fun driving through the Borders, along winding narrow roads with hills either side and spectacular scenery wherever you looked. Cattle grids kept sheep and cows within certain boundaries, but they still wandered all over the road and had no fear of cars. They just stood there, blocking the road and chewing the cud. Horns had no impact; you just had to be patient.

Beyond Peebles, the landscape changed and opened out. The Pentland Hills came into view, and the southern outskirts of the city of Edinburgh not long afterwards. The contrast between the rural peace of the Eskdale valley and the noise and busyness of the city was striking, but it was a welcome contrast.

By lunchtime, we'd completed much on the shopping list and stopped for a bite to eat. But at around 1 o'clock, I began to feel very strange indeed. Heavy and tired, my body felt as if it was grinding to a halt, and my energy was disappearing into a hole inside. This sensation didn't ease with the respite of food or drink, but seemed to be getting worse. Knowing I had to drive back to the monastery, I mentioned to Yangdak that I wasn't feeling so well and asked if we could go back. No problem, he said.

Driving back to Samye Ling, these sensations intensified, and I was struggling to stay focused. Tiredness seeped into every bone in my body, and my head felt heavy and devoid of any useful thoughts. It wasn't particularly unpleasant, but it didn't feel normal at all. By the time we reached Samye Ling, I was both grateful we'd made it and absolutely exhausted. I climbed out of the car, heading straight for my room, where I fell to my knees and crawled over the threshold. I collapsed on the floor and just lay there, with wave after wave of a deliciously blissful feeling superseding the tiredness. As this continued, I was dimly aware of the thought *Someone must be here,* before falling into a deep and peaceful sleep.

The next day, I went to breakfast as usual in the old Dining Room. Conversations were more animated than usual, and I picked up that Akong Rinpoche had returned from Tibet.

"When did he get back?" I asked.

"Yesterday lunchtime," came the answer.

I stopped and stared, remembering that it was at that time that I'd begun to feel so strange in Edinburgh. Lying on the floor, I'd been reminded of the peaceful, blissful state I'd been left in after my dream about Jesus, and I was very curious. Could this otherworldly state have been caused by the return of Rinpoche? Did this mean that I had a meaningful connection with him? It was time to find out.

After meditation, I made my way as usual to the Tea Rooms for the morning shift. Samye Ling was then—as it had been for years, apparently—something of a building site, and Phase Two of the Temple courtyard was in the planning. Over in the corner, I spotted a middle-aged Tibetan of short stature, wearing casual clothes, walking slowly around the building site in the company of two others.

I don't know what I was expecting, but in my more imaginative moments, I'd wondered if I might see rainbows dancing through him, or if time would stop and the world as I knew it would collapse into a colourful assembly of random shapes and colours, only to reform as a heavenly paradise.

Nothing happened. Not only did nothing happen, but he didn't even see me, let alone recognize me, and the joyful reunion between long-lost friends that I'd also ventured to anticipate evaporated like a dewdrop in the sun. I wasn't sure whether I'd made everything up, or if this was a teaching designed to shatter my ego, lest I start feeling or claiming special status as a result of my earlier experience.

Well, I'm still free, I thought at last. *At least I don't have to suddenly do anything different or take on any particular responsibilities.* I was used to doing well at school and at work and was often fending off expectations, for fear of buckling under pressure as I'd done once before. The anonymity was a blessed relief, I realized. I could just be me, and no one paid much attention.

Nothing further happened with Rinpoche for several weeks. He was back, and I'd see him occasionally walking around Samye Ling. I heard from other Samye-Lingers that he was quite a force and presence, a man of few words. When he spoke it would cut through any nonsense and leave you naked and in touch with your innermost being if you ever went for an "interview" and dared ask his advice. He was described as an "immovable mountain", an emanation of the Medicine Buddha, one of the kindest people you could ever meet, and utterly fearless. And yet he always appeared so ordinary, understated in his dress and his manner, accomplishing endless activities and never in a hurry.

It took several weeks to pluck up the courage to go and meet him, but eventually I put my name down on the list. I no longer recall this first interview, except that Rinpoche said very little and sat like an immovable mountain! I was out of my depth, intimidated, and yet so incredibly, bizarrely happy to be in the same room, to be making contact personally.

In these early days, I had no conscious understanding of what a "guru" was and wasn't looking for one. In the Vajrayana tradition, the relationship between a teacher and student, guru and disciple, is fundamental to the path. It is through the teacher, often regarded as a direct representative of the Buddha himself, that not only are teachings given but also transmissions of sacred texts, deity "empowerments", and direct blessings.

Merging our mind with the mind of the guru can bring about fast transformation, direct experience of the true nature of mind, and many other positive benefits. It is therefore of vital importance that such a teacher is trustworthy, pure, and part of a genuine lineage that can be traced back to the Buddha. These are just some of the safeguards to look for when investigating the authenticity of a potential teacher to whom one might become devoted.

It is clear that such a relationship can leave followers wide open to abuse and exploitation, as well as to an unhealthy abdication of responsibility for one's own life. Sadly, there are a number of instances where people in positions of authority, spiritual or otherwise, take advantage of those in their care. Buddhism is no exception, and this is in part why the advice given is that a potential student thoroughly "tests" a teacher for many years before asking to be taken on as a student.

Rinpoche didn't consider himself a guru or a teacher and wasn't looking for students or disciples. This made it difficult to understand what the relationship might be, and since I was unfamiliar and uncomfortable with notions of surrendering to the guru, I was quite happy to get to know him just as he was. If he gave teachings, I'd usually go. When he gave empowerments, I'd always try to be there. Occasionally I'd ask for an interview, increasingly wanting to be near him and believing, quite wrongly, that asking for his advice about my life was the way to show respect, humility, and my wish to be closer.

In truth, I was more like a child looking for a father, and I think Rinpoche knew this. He was immeasurably kind, always striking just the right balance between offering support and refusing to let me get too dependent. Frequently, his life advice was the antithesis of what I felt I wanted or could imagine, and was always an enormous stretch. I came out of several interviews brimming with enthusiasm, all set to follow his advice, which had seemed so do-able sitting in the room with him, only to sink into despair a few days later at the impossibility of the task ahead, which would then catalyze into fury at being given such an unreasonable mission!

Eventually, I would start laughing, and a profound letting go would take place. After this, I invariably found that I was quite content with the here-and-now. It took me a while to see how skilful Rinpoche's methods were, and how vast his wisdom!

Getting to know Akong Rinpoche more personally took a long time. I considered him my "root guru", a principal teacher with whom there was a particularly strong heart-connection, through whom much of the more intangible elements of the Dharma could be transmitted.

The Dharma, a Sanskrit word meaning "Truth", is both a formal body of Tibetan Buddhist scripture and the quintessence of what the Buddha's teaching is all about, manifesting in a myriad of ways.

Some of it can be learnt through study and reading or listening to teachings, but there is a very subtle aspect that cannot be gained through the intellect and cannot really be described in words, though receiving it is often referred to as a "blessing".

Blessings are experiential, transformative, occurring in ways that cannot usually be detected by the senses but nevertheless "liberate" the mind from wherever it's got bogged down, allowing one's true nature to be glimpsed, felt, and understood—often fleetingly but with enough reality to bring confidence, inspiration, enthusiasm, perseverance, and uplift in meaningful ways.

The Kagyu lineage, in which I was finding my Buddhist feet, is one of a number of schools of Tibetan Buddhism preserving an unbroken line of the Buddha's teachings for over 2,500 years. The Buddha himself first taught and "turned the Wheel of Dharma" in the Deer Park of Sarnath, near Varanasi in India. It was here that the Buddha taught The Four Noble Truths and laid the foundation for all the other teachings he subsequently gave.

No teachings were written down when the Buddha was alive and, in fact, Buddhism still has a strong oral tradition, relying on the living presence of teacher and student and verbal transmissions of text, discourse, *doha* (spiritual songs), and empowerments. But gradually, beginning with what became known as the Pali Canon, teachings began to be written down, and nowadays most key texts can be found in print.

I was still finding my way with this new world of Tibetan Buddhism, when a visiting teacher arrived at Samye Ling. He came every year and was well loved. "Very accessible as a person, funny, and very knowledgeable" was how others described Ringu Tulku Rinpoche. *Perfect for a proper introduction to Buddhist teaching*, I thought. I was looking forward to meeting him and attending teaching sessions in the Temple.

It was his laugh that struck me more than anything, along with his wide, beaming smile—so different from Akong Rinpoche, who rarely smiled and seemed so serious much of the time. I immediately warmed to Ringu Tulku and soaked up the teachings. Ringu Tulku was very "unscary", and I felt at ease with him. He had been awarded the title of Khenpo in 1975 and that of Lopön Chenpo (Great Master) in 1983 and was a very erudite and skilled teacher. He was working through Jamgön Kongtrul's *The Treasury of Knowledge*, directly from the Tibetan, and I arrived in the middle of this long series of teachings from one of Tibetan Buddhism's largest and most essential texts

I was curious though. Everything about Buddhism could be said to focus on the ultimate goal of Enlightenment, that elusive state that is not a state and is impossible to describe but through which suffering comes to an end and the clear light of one's pure awareness radiates unobstructed. There seemed to be endless routes up the mountain—innumerable rules and regulations in one direction, absolutely none in another direction; extremely difficult to attain from one perspective, simple and right under one's nose from another. What was the truth? And how could Enlightenment produce teachers of such differing personalities and characteristics, if Enlightenment meant the disappearance of the ordinary self? Why didn't everyone become the same? Were they really "enlightened"? Had I got the wrong end of the stick?

Essentially, yes, I'd got the wrong end of the stick. But in truth, most of us do. The questions that arise are part of our journey of discovering what Enlightenment might mean, and they are fuel for a great fire that may, if we're lucky enough, eventually burn down the edifice of our constructed reality and free the mind completely. Until then, rather like a dog chasing its tail, discussions tend to go round and round in circles and leave us as caught in our thinking minds, as trapped now as when we first began.

That didn't stop me, however. I loved the teachings and asking questions and receiving answers that often stopped my intellect in its tracks and opened it into a wider, more expanded space. But in my private life, I was really struggling with my feelings and what was in danger of becoming a relationship with my monk friend. Confusion and suffering on both sides was amplifying, and it was becoming an untenable situation. After much soul-searching, I decided I had to leave Samye Ling. I was heartbroken but knew it was for the best.

So, in a bid to curtail this suffering, I packed my bags and left, free to return whenever I wished, but no longer enduring what had become a daily torment for both Yangdak and myself.

Chapter 6
Love and Exile

Up in Edinburgh, I had time and space to reflect a little on the six months at Samye Ling and see how much I had learned, how rich my experience had been, and how fortunate I was to have been able, at the eleventh hour and thanks to my karma, to stay. It was not lost on me that the greatest source of my then suffering was the relationship I had with my monk friend. Just as the Buddhist teachings proclaimed, my attachment and grasping were indeed causing me pain and suffering. In my naivety, I had hoped, believed even, that getting close to someone on a spiritual path would prevent all of this. I couldn't have been more wrong!

I was more grateful than ever for the teachings, and for Samye Ling as a place I could go to, to take part in some of the many courses and retreats that ran throughout the year. For a year, I lived out and visited on a regular basis. I grew stronger, more committed than ever to practising the Dharma and more balanced with regard to the emotional turbulence that had filled my days in the run-up to the decision to leave. In the light of this, I asked if I might return to Samye Ling in an "official capacity", applying to become a resident and volunteer worker. This time, my application was accepted and, joyfully, I moved back, taking a room in the residents' accommodation up at Garwald House.

Garwald was much loved by all who lived there; a big, rambling house halfway up a long dirt track whose potholes ensured no speeding and where the quiet of the night was only ever broken by the hooting of owls. I lost count of the shooting stars I'd see walking home in the winter after dark, when the skies were lit by a million twinkling jewels. I'd been given my job back in the Tea Rooms, and the half-hour walk up and down the track before and after my shift or prayers was always a joy, even when the weather was bad, which it often was!

I was happy to be with Yangdak again, but things had happened between us that created tensions, and I knew he'd been questioning whether or not to stay at Samye Ling. He felt torn between two very different lives, two parts of himself, and my presence back in the monastery seemed to bring things to a head. Quite abruptly, or so it appeared to me, he announced that he would be leaving and going back to live in Edinburgh and that I was being given the job of managing the Tea Rooms in his absence.

I was absolutely devastated—and furious! I had not anticipated this, and I neither wanted the responsibility of the job nor for him to leave, and I certainly didn't appreciate being dumped "with the baby", as I saw it, while he went off to the bright lights of the city, turning his back on everything to which he had been so committed . . . including me. But he had made up his mind and there was no changing his decision. He left, and I had to come to terms with it. It had been hard for us both to see each other's position and perspective, and we'd fallen out many times, our positive communication deteriorating into spats, huffs, and some spectacular scenes. Truth be told, there was great wisdom in his decision, but I didn't see it that way at the time!

Even Lama Yeshe seemed to take pity on me, as I moved through each day with so much heartache it was hard to get out of bed in the morning. I really had got attached! Very possibly, the abbot had seen all this coming, or had feared things would end badly, and perhaps this was why he'd tried so hard to prevent us getting too close.

I was eating a lot of humble pie and applying antidote after antidote to the wounds of my own creation, but I was also learning the power of compassion. The community showed great kindness, not judging—at least to my face—the very real and painful mess I'd got myself into. I wasn't the first to go through this experience in the monastery, and I wouldn't be the last. We were all so very human, looking for love and happiness and forging strong, close bonds within a fairly intense environment. It was inevitable that partnerships would develop and, although this was discouraged, particularly for those in robes, they happened. Some turned out well, others lasted only a short time, but they each had their natural lifespan.

Despite the enthusiasm the abbot had had for residents to "take robes", wishing as he did to build a resilient monastic community, over time the pedestal of the robes came under review. There were too many falling off the perch, and failing in a lifestyle that was asking too much, too soon. The abbot realized this, and the attitude towards encouraging newcomers to become monks and nuns changed. It would be a step taken only after serious consideration and after a much longer period of living in the community as a layperson.

Meanwhile, I was mopping up my own tears with every swill of the bucket that cleaned the floor of the Tea Rooms. But new friends were being made, and I could see that there was an opportunity I hadn't had before to find my place within the community. Slowly, my heart healed, and I began to enjoy myself again. It took a while to realize that it was because of one particular person that I'd begun to feel more cheerful.

And there I was, falling in love all over again, with a very different person, with whom I was sure, this time, it would all work out differently. We were responsible, mature, thoughtful, and kind towards each other and equally committed to the community at large. I had learned from my earlier mistakes and was determined that no one would get hurt or upset by this blossoming fondness and friendship. We spoke openly, respectfully, and honestly about everything and, after a few months, realized that we were serious and needed to take appropriate action. In our minds, the simplest solution was for him to renounce his robes and for us to be a couple in the community, continuing our work but within this new context. An interview with the abbot was organized, and Mikki went to see him.

* * *

I waited as if waiting for the results of a potentially life-threatening doctor's diagnosis. When he returned, I took one look at his face and knew it wasn't good news.

"Lama was furious. He says that if you and I get together, we must both leave Samye Ling, and we'll never be allowed to return."

Once more, I was in deep shock. "But why? We've not done anything wrong. This is such a positive relationship, which we've conducted with utmost respect for everyone likely to be affected. I don't understand this at all."

And I didn't. Neither of us did. We were upset and angry, feeling unfairly judged and harshly treated.

"I'm going to see Rinpoche," said my friend, whose devotion to Akong Rinpoche was deeper and more important than anything else in his life.

We knew that Rinpoche was invariably calm in the face of any situation, and we hoped that he might see things differently. Another interview was scheduled and, once more, I waited as if for a frightening diagnosis, but with more confidence this would turn out okay.

One look at Mikki's face, however, quickly told me otherwise, and I felt the earth falling away beneath my feet. He had tears in his eyes as he told me that Rinpoche's words had been like a knife in his heart:

"Rinpoche says you're not the right woman for me."

Stunned and disbelieving, I couldn't speak. I stared at him, knowing that Rinpoche's words were the death knell for our relationship and our future. He trusted Rinpoche with every cell of his body, and there was no going against his advice or insight. I also knew that in the light of this refusal, and having infuriated and once more upset the abbot, I would probably have to leave Samye Ling again.

I had very little money by this stage, having used the proceeds from the sale of my house to fund my time at Samye Ling and my "gap year" in Edinburgh. But I wasn't ready to return home to England. I realized that I had inadvertently made myself homeless, virtually penniless, and broken-hearted, with my reputation in shreds and my mind in pieces—all in the pursuit of love and enlightenment!

I decided to go north, up to Findhorn, another community I'd heard many good things about and one where I felt I might recover in. The pressure in my mind pushed me towards what felt like insanity. I had had such trust, love, and confidence in the Dharma, in God, I couldn't believe that I had got myself into this disastrous situation. I felt judged, persecuted, exiled, cast out, labelled an "evil woman trying to seduce monks and pull them off the path"—that was how it seemed that I'd been painted. But it felt so far from my inner truth and motivation that I simply reeled at the perceived injustice and wanted to get as far away from Samye Ling as I could.

In my heart and mind, it was nothing to do with that: the robes were wonderful, but there were human beings inside them who had feelings and who sometimes outgrew the robes, being ready to live the Dharma in another context, a household one of marriage and family. There was nothing wrong with that, I thought. It was natural. It could be equally positive and equally strong. Yes, there were challenges, but that wasn't a bad thing. What better way to overcome the pitfalls of attachment and aversion than by learning how to really love in a committed relationship?

All these thoughts and questions churned away day and night. I found no peace. At one point, the pain in my mind was so intense, I didn't know what to do. I wanted to get rid of it, to get away from it, but remembered the teachings about aversion to pain and how overcoming that aversion was the way to approach it—to "lean into it", not resisting but welcoming it.

So I turned towards the pain, leaned into it, and tried to relax. As I did so, a very bright light right in the centre of my brain seemed to switch on. I looked at it, and it grew brighter and stronger, and I began to feel much better. Most unexpectedly, the Dalai Lama's face came into view, radiating compassion and kindness towards me. I felt understood, seen, and forgiven. *I'm okay, and I'm going to be okay,* I thought.

This single incident took the worst of the suffering away, gave me peace, and somehow sanctified innocence in the core of my being. I'd never met the Dalai Lama, but he had heard my "cries of suffering" and like Chenrezig, the emanation of the Lord of Compassion that he was said to be, he had come to my aid. My faith in Buddhism was restored, and I knew that compassion was my way through. Compassion was the right response towards everyone in this scenario, and that included all those who judged, despised, or thought ill of me.

It was a huge lesson.

I'd had enough money for two nights in a bed-and-breakfast in Forres, the village surrounding Findhorn up in the northeast of Scotland. In chatting with the landlady, I'd explained that I was hoping to stay a little longer. I couldn't afford private lodgings, but I had a tent and wondered if she could recommend a site nearby. She suggested a spot, and I was preparing to head off, when she came up to me to say some friends in the village were going on holiday for three weeks and had been let down at the last minute by their house/cat-sitter. Would I like to step in? Without hesitation, I leapt at the invitation. What a gift! The perfect solution for both parties.

During this three-week period, I walked and walked around the beautiful bay of Findhorn and the countryside around the Moray Firth. I returned to visit Pluscarden Abbey near Elgin many times, sitting in the chapel and asking, praying, for guidance and that my heart be filled with the love and compassion Christ had shown me in the dream. I watched the monks walking mindfully in their white robes. Unlike most Benedictine communities, the monks at

Pluscarden wore white like the Cistercians. They were a Catholic Order, and one of the reasons they'd adopted the white robes instead of the customary black ones was to signify their special devotion to Our Lady.

I loved the monastery and the Gregorian Chant, Latin Mass, and had noticed the veneration towards Mary. Carrying the identity of a "condemned woman", I found great comfort in this devotion, and my attention was drawn to the Holy Mother and Mary Magdalene, the two women who had suffered most acutely in their love for Jesus.

I recalled a particular practice in Buddhism that I thought might help. It was called Tonglen and was known as a "compassion practice". The idea is that we take on the suffering of others and transform it through our compassion into liberation and happiness. Weighed down by our own suffering, it can feel like the last thing we'd want to do, or even should do, lest we sink into immobilizing despair or depression. But, counterintuitively, Tonglen has the reverse effect. So I tried it.

Settling myself into a meditation position, I closed my eyes and brought my attention to the heart where I imagined Jesus, Buddha, warmth, lovingkindness, and compassion all present. I couldn't pick one figure, so I let my mind move between them until the feeling of compassion was palpable.

I then imagined one of the people who'd brought me pain standing in front of me. Instantly, my body tightened, and my heart wanted to close, but I kept breathing, telling myself, "This person is also looking for love and happiness, just like me" until I could simultaneously feel the compassion in my own heart whilst holding the image of the other person steady. I then invited them to give me their pain, their anger, disapproval, whatever they held against me, and I breathed it into my heart as dark smoke. I let the figures of compassion and the pure feeling in my heart take in the smoke and then imagined bright, white smoke being offered in return as I exhaled. This white smoke then settled into the heart of the other person, and so the cycle of breathing and black–white smoke exchange continued until there was no more black smoke coming towards me. Remarkably, what was left was pure peace.

I continued with the Tonglen practice over and over, working with different people and sometimes just myself, externalizing the "suffering me" and inviting that part to give me her pain through breathing in black smoke. This worked, too! Of course, one round of the practice wasn't a permanent cure, but it was effective, and I noticed how much more compassionate I felt generally as the weeks passed, how much more accepting and joyful, even in the midst of what were fairly challenging circumstances.

I reflected on the heartbreak I'd brought upon myself through falling in love with not one but two monks. Not that I had any choice at the time, but it really was asking for trouble. Questions bubbled over. Was it the lure of the unobtainable man? Was it as much about the robes as the person? Did I unconsciously want to take robes myself but was just too scared? Was I secretly disrespectful of the monastic vows because I thought they were unnatural and suppressed aspects of our humanity that shouldn't be suppressed? Suppression that caused all manner of distortions and that might lead to abuse and a lot of unhappiness and suffering.

I looked at my own feminine nature. I perceived myself as loving, passionate, and kind-hearted, but when I looked more closely, I could also see how jealous I could be, how demanding and volatile—how strong my ego was. I had been shattered and devastated over and over, but what was shattered and devastated? Was it really "me"?

Since I also recovered, bouncing back like a ping-pong ball, as my mother used to say, I couldn't have really been as completely devastated as I felt at the time. So, maybe something else was going on; maybe it was my ego that was taking a bashing, and maybe this was even a good thing!

This dawning revelation brought a lightness and a complete change of perspective. Instead of feeling a "victim" of the situations I'd found myself in, I began to consider they might have all been blessings; clever scenarios dreamt up by the Enlightened Ones to bring about the breaking of the shell of my ego that would actually liberate me. Or perhaps my Higher Self had orchestrated all this. Or the clashing contradictions of my higher consciousness and lower instincts were locked in a kind of battle of good over evil and on this occasion, good was winning.

I considered the position I'd been in: a young woman, a spiritual seeker, who believed in marriage and sex, living in a mixed community of other young spiritual seekers, most of whom mistrusted relationship and had taken vows of celibacy. I was embarrassed to admit to myself that my strong belief in relationships and sex as a good thing, especially within a spiritually focused life, had driven me to think, speak, and behave in ways that were not fully respectful of the monastic vows.

I felt a lot of shame and confusion. It was clear that the vows were a prison for some people and seemed to create more shame around sex and sexuality than was already lurking in the unconscious of so many. But it was also true that for many, the vows were a deep and meaningful commitment to something greater than ordinary human impulses and that they were sacred and not to be treated lightly.

Thoughts turned again to the story of Mary Magdalene, the woman portrayed as a prostitute who'd been redeemed by Jesus after turning to him for help and who'd become one of his closest disciples. Or was it more? Was she, as the Bible stated, a penitent, fallen woman cleansed and purified through confession, renunciation, and conversion? Or was she, as others have argued, a highly trained temple priestess who became the wife and consort of Jesus, an equal in her own right—her union with him bestowing on her a special status that was at times resented by the other disciples?

What was the problem with the sexuality of a woman that meant it had to be controlled? Throughout history and across religion and cultures worldwide, women's sexuality has so often been the "property" of men. Why? Why was the sexuality of men controlled in so many religious contexts? The answer to that question seemed obvious, but it also pointed to this fundamental fear and shame at the root of our human experience. I became increasingly curious about this whole subject.

But first, there was the issue of homelessness. What was I going to do once the three-week cat-sit came to an end? There were a number of possibilities, but most of them seemed like admitting defeat, and I didn't feel defeated. Whilst bridges had been burned and doors had slammed, other doors had opened, and there was light on the path ahead. Several times, the memory of an invitation offered by a woman who lived in the Eskdale valley returned. She was setting up a small retreat centre and had asked if I might like to help. It was very close to Samye Ling, but far enough not to be on the doorstep, and independent. I got in touch.

The door opened. Rita would be delighted for me to come. She had a room ready, and we'd work things out as we went along. I was overjoyed. Here was a lovely old school house in the process of being converted into a retreat centre in the perfect location. The focus was on "the feminine", and I was encouraged to be "who I was". I was also sufficiently close to Samye Ling to continue my Buddhist practice and deepen my true understanding of what it was really all about. And to see my monk friend—it wasn't "over" between us, as far as I was aware, and I was keen to work it through without losing our actual friendship.

* * *

At the end of the stay in Findhorn, I drove south, heading to my new home in the Esk Valley with my few possessions and a heart of gratitude and joyful enthusiasm. Before leaving, though, I decided to make a visit en route to a most unusual place I'd heard about at Pluscarden Abbey: the Sancti Angeli Skete.

Chapter 7
The Feminine Face of God

I'd never heard of a skete. In fact, there are very few left on either side of the Eastern/Western Christian divide, but tucked away in the Glen Affric Highlands of Scotland was a tiny skete called Sancti Angeli.

A skete is a semi-hermitage, a small gathering of hermits you could say, who live alone but come together for one or two Offices a day and share resources and mutual support if needed. It was one of the earliest forms of monasticism in the Christian Church, possibly started in Egypt in the Scetis Valley, where skete communities first appear. Seen as a bridge between full community life and the total isolation of hermit life, it was popular in these early years but fell out of favour by the Middle Ages. This was due mainly to a growing need at that time for greater physical safety.

Fast-forward to the 20th century and the remarkable story of one Catholic Sister who had been granted a papal indult to have her monastic training at St. Cecilia's Abbey in Ryde on the Isle of Wight. For many years, she had been drawn to the ancient monastic tradition of solitary life, and the Benedictine sisters at Ryde helped her prepare for it. Her wish was eventually granted when the then Bishop of Aberdeen offered her the use of a vacant presbytery in the Highland village of Cannich, near Loch Ness, for the project. Sister Petra Clare took up the invitation and, together with another sister, she relocated several hundred miles north to the much harsher climate but relative isolation of the Scottish Highlands. They developed a monastic skete, where she had lived, usually alone, for 15 years.

Sister Petra Clare was also an iconographer of some repute. Her work was beautiful, and I'd been struck by two large icons in Pluscarden Abbey that she had painted, or "written": one of St. John the Baptist and the other of St. Andrew. Her style was similar to the Eastern Orthodox icons I had seen in a number of places, but it also had Romanesque features. Her icons shone with beauty, artistic skill, fine materials, and something else that is hard to describe or "locate" in the two-dimensional image staring at you but which seems to come forth from a hidden dimension.

I was fascinated by the process of making icons: the devotional state of mind of the iconographer as much as the discipline of technique, both of which seem to act as a conduit for divine light to imbue the canvas and reach through into our very soul.

* * *

Arriving at Sancti Angeli, I was greeted by a vivacious, warm, and friendly nun dressed in the Benedictine habit. I always expected hermits to be quiet, retiring people who shunned human company, but the few whom I had met were quite the opposite. Sister Petra Clare showed me to my simple room, my cell, and set about instructing me in the conventions of life in the skete.

The emphasis was on mindfulness—not that the concept of mindfulness was part of our everyday language, let alone daily life, in the late 1990s, but this was the way every action was approached and undertaken under Sister Petra Clare's joyful, loving, and expert tuition: slowing down, letting the mind settle, and paying attention to the present moment and its activity with clear, undistracted awareness.

In particular, I remember learning about the "monastic cup of coffee". Whilst drinking a cup of coffee, there is nothing else to think about or do. The kettle boils, and water is poured into two pottery bowls, where coffee grains instantly dissolve, turning the pure water to a brown, murky, slightly frothy liquid. The spoon is stirred and patterns on the surface of the liquid come and go like ripples on a lake. Milk is carefully added, according to preference. With both hands, you take hold of the bowl, noticing the rough texture against the hands, the brackish colour of the hot liquid, and the steam snaking its gossamer path upwards. You catch the aroma of roasted, bitter coffee as it wafts past the nose. You sit slowly and mindfully at the table and give thanks prayerfully before lifting the bowl to the lips and savouring the first sips of what is fast becoming an elixir of the gods before your very eyes. Never has a cup of instant coffee tasted so very fine!

As I got to know Sister Petra Clare a little better, I began to sense that the way she lived her monastic life was integral to the way she approached iconography. By slowing down and being mindful and present, every action was imbued with divinity. So, whether that was reciting the Psalms, drinking coffee, or picking up a paintbrush, an intimate relationship with God was always at the centre. Having seen Sister Petra Clare's icons at Pluscarden Abbey, I hoped to learn more about her work and perhaps to see an icon in the process of being written, so I was delighted to be invited in to her studio. Any artist's studio is sacred space and of course this was no exception: modest and clean, with a lot of light, there was the familiar sight of "canvases in waiting" and other tools of the trade. What caught my eye though were the emerging contours of a face on an otherwise blank canvas. Rendered somewhat impersonal by the traditional style and yet looking so directly and personally into my being, I wondered about the mysterious power of an icon. I asked Sister Petra Clare if she could put this into words. This is what she said:

> According to tradition, the icon "makes present" Christ, Mary, the angels, and saints. It is not, of course, Christ or a saint. It is a piece of painted wood, but the painter, and hopefully, the viewer, is looking

> towards the holy person who is depicted in the icon. If you look at a photo of Grandma, you recall to mind the presence of that person. Because Christ is God and man, and, according to the fathers, "God became man so that man might become god"—that is, *divinized*, made divine by participation—the icon is painted in a special way to demonstrate these properties. Because God is beyond human perception and understanding, while man is physical, in three dimensions, the icon technique is a conversation between the abstract—the non-natural and the natural—and partakes of both characteristics. The abstract elements of the icon prompt the human to go beyond him/herself, and desire to be united with God, which is the true destiny and eternal happiness of any person.

My stay at Sancti Angeli was very joyful and reignited my relationship with Christianity, which had inevitably fallen somewhat by the wayside whilst I was so fully immersed in Tibetan Buddhism at Samye Ling. I'd been confused to find myself in a tradition so far from my own, particularly having been led there by Jesus himself—or at least my wish to become like him, to become the person I'd experienced myself to be in that fateful dream. Theologically, the two faith traditions bear little resemblance to each other, and directly contradict each other in places. This is what had confused me and led to periods of real mental anguish as my loyalty to Christianity was challenged over and over.

My actual experience, though, was that each seemed to offer an equally valid path to the Divine, to our inherent spiritual potential and core being. Through the contemplative, mystical paths in both traditions, I began to see that God was the "same thing"—not a thing at all, of course, and certainly not a person. God had many names but seemed to me to be more like a shift in one's consciousness than anything else; a shift whereby the ordinary sense of oneself fell away and the natural light of pure awareness, a more transcendent and yet intimate and authentic experience of "self", was simply revealed.

My glimpses were fleeting and not very bright, but they were real enough for my whole understanding of God to change and for me to see that my experience of life tended to twist and turn according to my own mind far more than it did to the outer circumstances I so often saw as the "cause" of whatever I felt or thought.

* * *

Having found once more a keen sense of wellbeing and inherent "goodness", I was ready to take up the new position at the small retreat house. I ventured south, back to the Scottish Borders, noting the heightened wakefulness as I approached the orbit of Samye Ling. I wouldn't think about it, I decided. Approach the valley with the spirit of a monastic cup of coffee.

The simplicity of the Sancti Angeli skete was good grounding for my new role at the retreat house, where there was no adherence to any particular faith. A painting of a Swiss hermit and saint, Bruder Klaus, hung on one wall, whilst a Buddha sat in the garden, but the tone and style of the retreat house was more Zen than anything, and I welcomed its open spaciousness.

My room was sparsely furnished but cheerfully painted, overlooking low hills with their flocks of white sheep grazing and a fast-flowing stream outside my window. Meditation formed the spiritual structure of the day, and I quickly settled into this new home, finding affinity with Rita and enjoying many conversations shared over mealtimes. Much of our time was in silence, and I was grateful for the freedom and space this gave.

* * *

After a couple of weeks, it was time to make a return visit to Samye Ling. I was nervous but excited to go back and walked the short mile and a half journey to the monastery along the road, noticing the sharp contrast between the gentle, feminine space of Rita's retreat house and the strong masculine presence of the Tibetan monastery and centre.

Through the entrance and past the new butter lamp house with its candles flickering through the windows and the rows of small stupas, symmetrical monuments built with specific proportions said to balance the elements and housing relics or statues of the Buddha. I had a cup of coffee in the Tea Rooms and then a wander in the gardens, where herbs and vegetables were growing in abundance. I looked up to see two monks coming towards me and greeted them with smiles.

"Could we speak to you?" they asked, both somewhat formal in their manner.

"Of course," I said.

I walked with them into the greenhouse, sensing something was amiss and becoming a little uneasy.

"We've decided as a community that you're no longer welcome at Samye Ling, and we're asking you to leave and not to come back."

Not for the first time, I listened to these words in stunned silence. I couldn't find any words and just looked at them; one angry face and one sheepish face. I knew them both and felt sorry that it had befallen the second monk to carry out what looked like reluctant orders for him. But there I was: being asked to leave again!

I had left on my own initiative on the two previous occasions, albeit with swords of Damocles hanging over my head, so was completely unprepared for this unexpected expulsion. I was accompanied to the gate, each step a strange dancing mirage of a "walk of shame" that merged with a pleasant stroll in the company of two brothers in robes.

In shock, I carried on walking back to my new home. Worlds swam before my eyes, the old trauma of rejection, judgement, and exile reasserted its grip, and I was once more floundering in thoughts and feelings I could neither control nor understand. What *was* this karma? Why did this keep happening, and what was I truly supposed to do about it?

I didn't feel like taking it lying down, so I determined to go back and speak to the abbot to find out if this decision had come from him or from the community itself.

"It hasn't come from me," he informed me. "But I suggest you stay away for three months to let things settle down and then begin to come back slowly if you want."

He was right. This was the best advice, and I thanked him, grateful that he no longer held me in the poor light he once had and happy to stay away out of respect for others' feelings and wishes.

* * *

The cut-off from Samye Ling was hard, but it was also a blessing. It offered some space and the chance to focus on the work with Rita without being pulled in different directions, as well as an enforced and prolonged separation from my friend. He was struggling as much as I was with the situation we found ourselves in, but he'd taken Rinpoche's words to heart, and there was no changing his mind, whatever his feelings might have been. It was better, therefore, not to see each other and not get more entangled. I missed him, but I couldn't fight forces that were so much stronger than either of us. I had to let go.

Sinking into the peace and relative solitude of the Tara House was healing—there was a homeliness and intimacy there. Leaving my home in Oxfordshire to live in a large community without any real security, then being rejected by the place I'd given so much up for, was very painful, and I needed time to come to terms with all that had happened. I regretted nothing, but things had hardly gone as I'd imagined or hoped!

I kept thinking of Mary Magdalene and the many ways in which women had been subjugated, cast out, condemned. For what? I was curious about the differing versions of who Mary Magdalene really was: priestess or whore? I knew that, even today, women who were sexually free could be written off as cheap, sluttish, and immoral. And yet, in the past, women had known their sexual power and, through training and ritual, had offered their bodies as temple priestesses to men who paid for their services. But this was a sacred act, not a commercial transaction; a highly revered practice, not a degrading exchange that emptied the soul of the woman.

Like so many girls of my generation, I was brought up to think women were somehow secondary to men in importance. We hoped for husbands who'd love and provide for us, even whilst we were educated and given every possible opportunity to make good careers and have a place in the world alongside these men. There was plenty of discrimination still, much of it hidden or simply accepted as the norm, but there was change happening, and my generation of women had far more freedoms than our mothers had.

It was a revelation to start looking into the role of women within a spiritual context, both throughout history and into the modern era—the end of the 20th century, as it was then. I'd never questioned the status quo, accepting as I did the authority of whichever institution I was a part of. I could see that most were fundamentally patriarchal, ensuring women and the feminine principle were kept at a safe distance and not given too much power. But my own experience had forced me to confront ideas and attitudes that were damaging, ill informed, and outdated, and to see the cracks in a system that was seriously out of balance and in need of reform and radical change.

There was an inner revolution going on, and it led me to start asking similar questions about Tibetan Buddhism. Where, I asked myself, were the women in Tibetan Buddhism?

Part Two

Tara and the Peace Pilgrimage

Chapter 8
Starting Out

There is an expression most of us will be familiar with: "to be hidden in plain sight". How often do we find that, when we are ready for something, it appears right in front of us, often having been there all along? This is exactly what happened once I started to ask questions about the nature of the feminine within Tibetan Buddhism.

Although there were, and still are, very few women who hold positions of spiritual or religious authority in Tibetan Buddhism, there is one figure that is absolutely central to the understanding and practice of what is called the Dharma, the body of teaching given or inspired by the Buddha—and that is Tara.

Said to be the "Mother of all the Buddhas", Tara represents the feminine principle from which all phenomena manifest and into which all phenomena will eventually disappear. As such, Tara can and needs to be understood on several levels, from the most subtle and esoteric to the most obvious and mundane. Tara may be conceived of as a kind of cosmic creative force, or she may be identified within the loving earthly mother who cares night and day for her ailing child, filled only with a selfless compassion and a willingness to do whatever is necessary to help her child.

This feminine principle is found not only in women but also in men and all sentient beings. It is the other half of the equation within us all that allows the cycles of life and death. Once this is understood, it makes no sense at all that the feminine should ever have been, or continues to be, regarded as somehow "less than" the masculine.

It baffled me that the deep devotion that Buddhist practitioners had for Tara did not translate into cultural norms or everyday attitudes, but once I started to focus on Tara these inconsistencies faded into the background. I began to discover just what is possible when we develop a relationship with a being such as Tara—though I hesitate to use the term "being", as she is ultimately beyond any description or personification we might come up with.

It is because of this perhaps that Tibetan Buddhism depicts such beings as deities. They are not inherently human; that is, made of flesh and bone (though they may take this form); rather, they are rainbow-like in their appearance, insubstantial, full of light, portals between the invisible world of pure undifferentiated consciousness and the visible, tangible world of matter. As such, the deity in Tibetan Buddhism is a very important figure, as it becomes a key for awakening or revealing the enlightened mind. There are thousands of deities, and Tara is but one in a pantheon, but each one is pointing to the same thing in the end: the naturally enlightened state.

So how does this work? How can focusing on Tara, for example, facilitate this change in our consciousness?

There are many ways to understand or describe who or what Tara (or any deity) is. Her most essential nature is hard to put into words, because it's beyond concept. It is the source from which all form comes and into which it returns. In this way, Tara is the unborn, uncreated "is-ness" that mystics throughout history have recognized as the indestructible essence at the heart of everything, including ourselves.

But forms manifest, or appear to manifest, from this "emptiness" and have what might be called a "vibrational frequency". A very high vibrational frequency might not be possible to see with our human eye, but it might still be present and actively affecting our consciousness or body. I tend to think of a deity in this way; rather like an angelic presence, though not always angelic in nature.

Some deities are peaceful, but some are wrathful, although they are all manifestations of compassion. How much they are simply a sophisticated projection of our own pure mind, and how much they have an "autonomous reality" is an interesting question in itself, but certainly, when I first discovered Tara, she seemed to have an independent reality that I could touch and even merge with that was not "me".

Tara is probably the most popular of all the female deities, and she is most commonly recognized in one of two forms: Green Tara and White Tara. There are, however, many forms of Tara, each differing slightly in their qualities and appearance, but they are all essentially emanations of the one central figure of Tara.

We will explore the qualities of both Green and White Tara, but for now continue with a generalized understanding of Tara and the value of deity practice when it comes to awakening our greatest potential. Praying to or meditating on a deity is a powerful way to bring alive the deity's qualities within our own minds.

As these qualities are an integral part of our consciousness, when we focus on them, we activate them. The deity is like a mirror, reflecting our own potential back to us. This is why human individuals may also be described as an emanation of a particular deity. Someone who has "realized" the oneness of their own nature with that of a deity may be said to have "become the deity".

There are many stories of Tara appearing in human form as a woman, the most famous one within the Buddha's teaching being that of the story of Princess Wisdom Moon.

In this story, it is the era when the Drum Sound Buddha was living and teaching in a land called Multicoloured Light. In this land there was a king, whose daughter Wisdom Moon was a devoted follower of the Buddha and had become a great practitioner in her own right—so much so that the monks were impressed and encouraged her to pray for a male rebirth so that she could be of benefit to beings and advance her spiritual progress.

Her reply was not what anyone expected, but it revealed how deep her realization already was: "Here, there is no man; there is no woman, no self, no person, and no consciousness. Labelling "male" or "female" is hollow. Oh, how worldly fools delude themselves."[3]

She then vowed to always be reborn in a female body to help lead beings to liberation beyond suffering and to counteract the ignorance of those who believed being born in a male body was better. Wisdom Moon stood against the patriarchy of the time and opened the way for a new respect and appreciation of women and the female form. She also gained the name of Tara, meaning "Saviouress" in Sanskrit, such was her commitment, compassion, and tireless activity in serving and saving beings.

* * *

How curious that she had been here all along, and I'd never really noticed. It had taken so much suffering, such exposure to the realities of my "wounded feminine" for me to seek out examples of a more enlightened feminine. And here she was—Tara. Radiating her unconditional love, she was suddenly everywhere!

Then, in 2005, my father died. It wasn't sudden, as he'd been unwell for several years, but still it was unexpected. Nothing quite prepares us for the death of a parent, and grief rolled into my life with an unprecedented force. I turned to my practice and my connection with Tara more strongly than ever, finding great comfort in it.

As the awareness of the impermanence of life and our most precious relationships sank in ever deeper, so I itched once more to do something that might be of benefit to others and that might also help transform my sadness and grief into something positive and life-affirming at the same time.

It wasn't long before an idea began forming. It seemed a little crazy, but at the same time filled me with inspiration and a strong feeling of purpose: I would do a Peace Pilgrimage with Green Tara as the focus, and I would endeavour to take Tara anywhere in the world where her particular activity of protection might be needed. As with many bright ideas, this one began with a vision that was vast and details that were vague!

Green Tara is often depicted as a central figure surrounded by 21 emanations; an emanation being a manifestation of Tara with the same essence as the original but associated with a specific activity and with an appearance that may be quite different at first glance. Some emanations appear fierce, as their energy may be what is required to subdue strong negative forces; others may be serene, with qualities better suited to supporting healing or spiritual development.

It made sense, therefore, to work with each emanation in turn, to get to know her qualities, to discover where she might be needed in the world, and then to "take her there". In practice, what that meant initially was to find out as much as I could about each of the 21 emanations of Tara.

This wasn't as easy as I had expected. Not only were there several different practice lineages of Tara but there wasn't much information about them, either. The 21 Praises to Green Tara are recited throughout monasteries, and often in private households as a daily practice, but although they are powerful and beautiful, each Tara is only described in a brief stanza.

I had found some inspiring images of the 21 emanations, so I decided to create some cards and meditate on these. I would get to know each emanation by doing the traditional Green Tara *sadhana* practice and, after completing it, sit quietly in meditation and focus on each particular emanation: seeing that Tara's appearance clearly, bringing to mind her attributes, and invoking her presence through reciting the Tara mantra: *Om Tare Tuttare Ture Soha.*

At some point, and this might take days, weeks, or even months, I would receive clear inspiration and guidance as to where she should be placed. I rejected the idea of sending the cards around the world.

Instead, I decided to buy 21 tiny statues of Tara that were no bigger than my thumb, ask Rinpoche if he would bless them, and I would then take them to wherever in the world they could be of benefit. A blessed statue, "consecrated" for its specific spiritual purpose, would carry the energy of Tara within it and allow her protection and healing to be physically manifested in different places.

It was a very big mission, but I was lit up! I had very little money, but enough to get started, and sometimes that's all that matters. It set in motion a series of synchronicities and opportunities that truly felt like Tara in action. If ever I'd questioned the relevance of Buddhist practice on the cushion to real life, which I most certainly had done, the Tara Pilgrimage confirmed for me not only how powerfully Buddhist practice could tame the mind but also how visibly the external world could be "moulded" by our practice—or perhaps, how inseparable the inner and outer realities really are.

The Tara Pilgrimage

Beginning

Monday 15 May 2006

It's pouring with rain here in Edinburgh, but the leaves on the trees are so lush and the air is dripping with the unfolding of new life. I am planning—preparing for the trip that begins at the end of this month. Not knowing where I'm going or how it's going to unfold.

This is a journey of inspiration. You know that wonderful experience when your mind is quite calmly doing its own thing and then *whoosh!* some bright idea pops in and you feel a great upsurge of energy. So easy to dismiss these moments, but when I'm free enough to pay attention, they become clues on a path, lights in the darkness of the unknown.

This is a mad idea really. "Set out from home base in Edinburgh, leaving everything behind, and take with you 21 small statues of Tara, a camera, a notebook, and your passport. Take the Taras to wherever in the world you are 'instructed' to go. Instructions will come through spiritual practice, intuition, and coincidence. Have complete faith and live the journey with the intention of doing 'Tara's Will'." Those were my clear guidelines.

My journey began with a White Tara who is peaceful and brings harmony whilst protecting from disasters.

Tara Enhancing Harmony

St. Cuthbert's Isle, Lindisfarne

Monday 22 May 2006

Most years I pay a visit to Holy Island Lindisfarne, in the most north-easterly corner of England. I set off there for the week and, quite unexpectedly, realized that this was going to be the beginning of the Tara trail.

It was here that two remarkable men came to teach the Christian message in the 7th century: Aidan and his successor, Cuthbert. The Northumbrian folk of the time were considered "barbarians" and had rejected all previous attempts to be converted to Christianity, but Aidan, an Irish monk sent out from Iona in Scotland, had been successful in his mission and had established a flourishing religious community on Lindisfarne. It was Cuthbert, however, who made the greatest impression on the people and who, even today, attracts pilgrims from far and wide. His story was written down by the great Benedictine scholar Bede, and this is why we know so much about him today.

As a young man, Cuthbert worked as a shepherd on the mainland across from Lindisfarne. One night he had a vision where angels appeared to come down from the sky and then return heavenward, carrying something in their wings. Cuthbert was later to discover that Aidan had died that night, resting against the walls of Lindisfarne Priory, and when he was told of this, he felt sure that this was who he'd seen being taken up to heaven.

Cuthbert's conversion and resolve were immediate. He went straight to Melrose Abbey, where he announced his intention to become a monk and commit his life to Christ. The abbot of Melrose, a man named Boisil, welcomed him warmly, discerning at first glance an unusual potential in this young monk.

Sadly, Boisil died when the plague that was spreading rapidly throughout the country made its way to Melrose Abbey, but Cuthbert was spared. He left the abbey and came to Lindisfarne, where he was made abbot soon thereafter. He was greatly loved and respected by the people and the Church and widely regarded as devout, gentle, steadfast, and strong. Stories recount how he would stand all night in prayer, with his feet in the sea, ankles warmed by otters emerging from the freezing waters.

As his popularity grew, Cuthbert began to yearn for greater solitude and privacy—not so much to retreat from the world but to draw closer to God and God alone. His first hermitage was built on a small part of the island that was cut off by the tide for several hours each day. Known as St. Cuthbert's Isle, it looks out over the mainland and the Farne Islands, which would become his home in later years.

Wednesday 24 May 2006

It's on St. Cuthbert's Isle that I placed the first Tara. This particular Tara is peaceful—white in colour and serene in countenance. She brings harmony and eases suffering through peaceful means. This island is a haven of natural peace and this, together with its rich spiritual heritage, seems an appropriate home for this Tara.

In leaving her here, I reflected on the personal significance of this site for my own spiritual awakening, which happened through Christ when I was in my 20s. Lindisfarne was one of the first places I came to on retreat, and I feel a sense of home here that has never changed. Truly it's a place where "the veil between God and Man grows thin". It has effortlessly pulled me into an inner experience of God that has given peace, joy, inspiration, direction, and faith.

My interest in Buddhism was not through disillusionment with Christianity, but through wanting to go deeper into the mysteries of faith and to find a way to get back to that experience that had changed my life.

When I first encountered the Buddhist teachings, and particularly the more mystical Vajrayana or Tantric school, it struck me that the state of bliss I had experienced was not dissimilar from the experience of enlightenment that Buddhism spoke about: the end of suffering, the flowering of our full potential as a human being. But in the Dharma, there were specific methods, a very clear path, and highly qualified teachers and spiritual adepts, all of which could support and guide me on this quest.

To some degree, I had to leave Christianity in order to follow the Buddhist path, as it was just too confusing to follow them both, but in my heart of hearts, I never completely left Christianity, because I could not deny or turn my back on that experience of meeting Christ—if that is what happened. It seemed appropriate, therefore, to remember and honour these roots by leaving Tara in a quintessentially Christian place.

Sitting in the ruined remains of St. Cuthbert's Hermitage, I was reminded of the unity of all faiths and the "marriage" of the masculine and the feminine, of our innate wholeness. It is so easy to focus too narrowly and become convinced that the path with which we resonate is the only true path. It may be the right path for one person, but that doesn't necessarily mean it's right for everyone. In the end there is no division, there is no conflict, no separation—all of that is human and born of our human condition. There is only the One Truth, and by whatever name it is called, through whichever traditional it is sought, I really believe it is the same truth, with the same essence. We are wise to remember our equality and our sameness, even as we celebrate our differences and diversity.

Tara Protection against Earth-Caused Disasters

Isle of Skye, Scotland

Tuesday 30 May 2006

I'm leaving Edinburgh at the weekend. I seem to "leave home" on a fairly regular basis and am almost getting used to being homeless! But the next Tara will be placed in Scotland.

The second Tara protects from earth-related disasters and from the negative emotion of pride. Because of the nature of interdependence, it is said that nothing in the external world exists separately from us, and all the Taras are described as simultaneously protecting us from external and internal forces of destruction and suffering.

Earth-caused disasters in the form of earthquakes, volcanoes, landslides are obvious, but it could be argued that what we are all facing now, as climate chaos increases, is an earth-related disaster on a massive scale. It is hard perhaps to see the link between human activity and shifting tectonic plates deep within the earth's structure, but not so hard to see the direct link between the burning of fossil fuels, increased carbon dioxide levels, and global warming, leading to melting ice caps, rising sea levels, enlarged areas of desert, severe drought, dying vegetation, and on and on. If we are caught in a negative state of pride, believing in a kind of Western capitalist superiority, refusing to see how damaging our actions can be, refusing to accept what's happening, and refusing to see that we need to change, then we are directly contributing to the death of the planet—and ourselves in the process.

During the travels with the second Tara, I'll be exploring and finding out more about what's happening to our planet and the things we can do—and are already being done—to restore the balance and bring us back into harmonious relationship with our home. Perhaps leaving the safety and security of a physical home in bricks and mortar will open my eyes to the deeper relationship I have, we all have, with this planet as home.

Wednesday 31 May 2006

Musings

I woke up feeling nervous this morning, which usually makes me want to hide or run away! However, I realized this was an opportunity to take a good look into the nature of anxiety and fear; after all the very essence of Tara is protection from fear.

In many spiritual teachings, I've heard the same message that there are really only two forces at play within us: love and fear. Love is our true nature, and fear is everything else, created and sustained by our ego.

The fundamental problem within the human condition is our belief in ourselves as an independent, self-existing, fixed "I", which we need to feed, clothe, look after, provide entertainment for, protect from pain, and steer towards pleasure. We believe we are responsible for the survival of this self, and this self believes its survival is what matters most. We become very attached to this idea of who we are and what we believe is good for us, and averse to what we believe is harmful.

This is all very sensible at face value. However, if we consider the consequences of millions of separate "I"s on the planet trying to secure their individual survival and happiness, there are many reasons why this perspective and behaviour becomes problematic. When resources are abundant, there is more likely to be relative harmony among individuals, but when resources are threatened or run out, competitiveness and conflict increase. If I believe that I need all these things to survive, then I am going to be afraid if I don't have them—and resent you if you do have them. This seed of aggression towards you may grow until I truly believe I have to get rid of you somehow, or steal from you, in order to protect my own interests.

Even in times of abundance, because of this drive to live according to the ego's belief system, my needs may just grow and grow until yesterday's luxury has become today's necessity. Greed spirals out of control until we are living in a kind of madness, obsessed with materialism, consuming all the time, blaming everyone "in power" for not giving us what we want or for what goes wrong—and perhaps discovering, for all that we have, we are still rather miserable. We are no longer able to see or care that half the world's population may be dying through famine and disease, aggravated at times by our own behaviours.

So fear is a big problem, acutely uncomfortable to experience and, therefore, hidden behind many other emotions, such as anger, pride, and jealousy. Fear makes us aware of our vulnerability and, without compassion or kindness, this can be really unpleasant.

But when I feel fear—raw fear—I am in touch with something in a more direct and naked way, and this seems to bring me closer to the truth of who I really am. I am vulnerable. I am subject to uncontrollable forces of change that include ageing, sickness, death, and losses of many kinds. Everything that exists is impermanent. So to rely on a false understanding, such as the one that the ego perpetuates, is dangerous and unwise. I suffer because of this, and contribute to the suffering of others.

When Buddhism talks of wisdom, it is referring to the state of innate "knowing", where the truth of existence and reality are clear to us and no longer obscured. The many methods and practices are designed to remove these obscurations, allowing our natural wisdom to shine forth.

Tara is the essence of wisdom, the embodiment of it, and with the dawning of wisdom, fear begins to dissolve. We see things the way they really are, and in this clear seeing, there is an understanding of who we really are and nothing left to be afraid of. I have faith in these practices, a lot of raw material to work with, and a sense of confidence that it really can be transformed.

Thursday 8 June 2006

The Quiraing

A few days ago, my friend Emma and I set off for the next leg of the journey. I'm on the road now, having packed up my things and left The Salisbury Centre, my home for the last couple of years. Travelling this first week with Emma wasn't scheduled, but since she had taken a week's holiday and was planning to go to the same part of Scotland at exactly the same time, we realized it couldn't be coincidence and decided to travel together.

After a long, cold spring, the warm, sunny weather we've had since we left is very welcome, and there are few places more beautiful than Scotland in the sunshine.

Heading north up the A82, we drove through Callendar, Crianlarich, stopping for a cup of tea brewed on the stove by a small lake before reaching Fort William in the late afternoon. Turning west, we drove towards Mallaig, where we could take the ferry the following morning for the Isle of Eigg. We'd been told to stay in Arisaig, three miles short of a real beauty spot with white sands and a hint of the Caribbean, so that's where we headed.

What we failed to appreciate, however, was the reason West Scotland is not, and probably never will be, overpopulated. Arriving at our campsite, preparing to erect the tent that had still not been out of its bag, the fog became the least of our problems as the dreaded Scottish midge homed in on its unsuspecting prey—possibly the entire population of West Scotland's midges, in fact. We'd wondered why there was no one around; they were all indoors.

I've never experienced a true plague of insects before. We screamed, swatted, and ran up and down, imitating a tribal dance to deflect the enemy's advances as we tried to pitch our tent for the night. Diving into the sleeping quarters as soon as they were up, we were then trapped, not daring to emerge again until the following morning. In her wisdom, Emma, a true Scot, had brought the only midge repellent known to protect soldiers on exercise on the Scottish west coast: Avon Skin So Soft. This cosmetic body oil is so wonderfully toxic that, as well as giving me asthma, it stopped the midges from feasting on succulent flesh, and I woke up with only three bites. Passing a less fortunate woman in the showers, I realized that the midge shows no mercy and Avon has done the world an unexpected favour.

The next morning, the fog took some time to clear, but when it did, we were rewarded with stunning views of the Small Isles and Skye. We took off for a spot of yoga down by the sea on brilliant velveteen white sands. We had decided, meanwhile, that Eigg was no longer a place to go; it was going to be Skye.

We duly took the ferry from Mallaig to Armadale and headed up the northeast coastline of Skye, along the Trotternish Peninsula and in the direction of Staffin. Little did I know how skilfully Tara was leading us. Beyond Portree, the peninsula begins, marked dramatically by a rock formation known as The Old Man of Storr.

* * *

Our hostel (forget camping!) was north of Staffin in a village called Flodigarry, directly opposite the Quiraing, a well-known destination for hikers. The hostel was an absolute jewel, once part of the four-star hotel next door and very comfortable indeed.

I'd been to the Quiraing before and had had one of those strange experiences of being transported to another time and place, so I knew it was a special place. J.R. Tolkien visited Skye as a child, and it's easy to see how such a landscape might have inspired the world that he created in *The Lord of the Rings.* What I didn't know was how the Quiraing had been formed, and I was curious. As luck would have it, a geology student had left a copy of her thesis investigating the origins of the rock formation in the hostel. As I began to read it, the fact we had ended up here began to seem nothing short of a miracle.

The Trotternish Peninsula is dominated by a lava escarpment that was subject to extensive failure during the Quaternary period, resulting in the largest and most spectacular landslides in the British Isles. The most impressive and dramatic of these is the Quiraing, which it seems is, to this day, relatively unstable, particularly around the Flodigarry area.

So here we were. Tara, whose particular activity is to protect from such earth-caused disasters, had brought us to the most relevant site in the UK.

The following day, we began the fairly difficult climb to the top of the Quiraing, our appreciation of the natural beauty greatly enriched by a recent knowledge of how it evolved and the awareness that millennia were embodied in the rocks beneath our feet. The geology student's study had revealed that the face of the escarpment was made up of two dominant lava types which, because they overlaid a much softer Jurassic type of clay, would have established unstable slope conditions. During the last Ice Age, glaciers flowed through this part of the world and settled here. This period was followed eventually by deglaciation, resulting in a significant weakening of the rock and causing a number of dramatic landslides to take place.

Walking through the landscape, we were struck by the way in which nature will take hold anywhere she can, and that life will continue at the first opportunity: The most delicate of flowers grew in obscure, remote, and barren parts of the escarpment.

After a two-mile walk, the path suddenly made a steep ascent, and we scrambled upwards along the path. We were heading for the Table, the very top of the Quiraing, at a height of nearly 600m. We were pretty much alone by this point, and the silence was eerie—simply us and the ravens and a rather wild wind. Reaching the magnificent green lawn on top of the mountain was a bit like finding paradise. We placed Tara in the ground there, close to a small stone circle, recited prayers, and our mission was accomplished.

Saturday 10 June 2006

Findhorn

Leaving Skye on Thursday, Emma and I planned to spend the night in Glenn Affric, but a road accident had blocked the road between Fort Augustus and our destination, so we were obliged to drive up the eastern side of Loch Ness and head straight to Inverness. Loch Ness lies along what looks like a geological fault line cutting across the northwest of Scotland. It's an eerie loch, no doubt about it. The depth of the waters gives it a dark, slightly sinister appearance, and its sheer size means that the waters get really quite choppy when the wind stirs.

We were heading to Findhorn on our journey anyway, so we decided to bring it forward and arrived late afternoon in what felt like the midst of a heat wave. Back to camping—and an altogether different experience this time!

Findhorn is a fascinating place, and very much somewhere to know about when it comes to investigating ways in which our future might be safeguarded on this planet. It began in 1962, when three people—Eileen and Peter Caddy and Dorothy Maclean—were guided to come and live in this part of the world. For six years, they shared a caravan and committed themselves to a simple, spiritually focused life guided by daily meditations that gave clear and specific instructions on how to realize their vision of a different way to live.

This vision led to what is now a world-renowned and innovative international community, always developing practical and ecological ways to ground spiritual ideals into everyday life. Thousands of volunteers have lent skills and time over the years, in particular with building projects. The buildings that are here today are testament to the possibilities of integrating ecological design and aesthetic beauty. There are straw-bale homes, homes built from huge whiskey barrels, and chalets with turf roofs. In the aptly named Field of Dreams, all the homes are built to a standard where insulation is ultra-efficient, solar panels are the norm, and water systems feed into the community sewerage system, which uses plants and natural filtration for decomposition and purification. All the electricity for the community is provided by three wind turbines.

It's an inspiring place—all the more so because it was one of the first of its kind. Eco-villages are springing up all over the world now and, with the emphasis on social/cultural harmony, spiritual practice, ethical business incentives, and ecological design, are fast becoming the way of the future. They offer a sustainable way of living on the earth that is peaceful, harmonious, creative, and enriching.

Thursday 15 June 2006
Pluscarden Abbey

Spending a couple of days at Pluscarden Abbey outside Elgin wasn't an obvious part of a Tara journey; it was more a case of "Well, I'm so close, I'd love to go back for a quick visit."

Pluscarden Abbey is the most northerly Benedictine monastery in the world. The monks here are part of the Valliscauldian Order, which was originally founded in France in an attempt to bring more austerity and simplicity to life in monastic communities. As such, they are similar in some respects to the Cistercians and the Carthusians, with a greater emphasis on silence, solitude, and discipline.

I love the Divine Office, and the very last of the day, Compline, concludes here with the most beautiful prayer to Mary, the Salve Regina. At Pluscarden, the Offices are still said in Latin, and the psalms are all sung in Gregorian chant. The whole experience is very moving, and the atmosphere in the chapel tangibly holy. Just walking through the doors, there is a heavy silence that hangs in the air, saturated with peace and with the kind of presence that automatically quiets the mind, stopping all attention from straying outside the purpose for which the chapel stands: prayer and praise to God.

* * *

Bearing in mind that this Tara also protects from suffering and sickness arising from the negative emotion of pride, I realized that such an environment was the perfect place to reflect on the value of humility and the problems of pride. In fact, St. Benedict himself stressed humility above almost all other qualities in the training for monastics. The chapter discussing the 12 steps of humility in The Rule of St. Benedict (which every Benedictine monastery follows and every monk or nun studies) is one of the longest and most detailed.

It's a hard one. It stresses, for example, that the abbot of a monastery must be regarded as God's direct representative and obedience to their instruction is essential and absolute for all monks and nuns. Such obedience mirrors the ultimate obedience to God that is the perfection of spiritual life. Knowing how difficult I personally find it to be told what to do, and in particular how to do it, I was reminded of the stubborn pride and ego that are a strong part of my own nature.

To surrender the individual will to God's will is the path of a monastic, and also the path of any spiritual aspirant. Reflecting on this, I spent a sleepless second night in a state of acute discomfort, dreading Mass the following morning and dreading the commitments I'd made for the rest of that day, all of which involved some level of surrender to the spiritual dimension. I was also in a lot of pain with my menstrual cycle, which had changed after my father died and seemed to be pushing me into a kind of surrender in its own way. My ego was in revolt and was clinging on for dear life. I couldn't get a sense of what it was clinging to, but since every muscle in my body was rigid, I knew I was terrified of something.

I've experienced this before, many times, and it's always been when something much more powerful than me is inviting me in. I know it's a blessing, but the unconscious resistance is huge each time, and that communicates itself as fear. So when the Bible talks of the "fear of God", I understand it! It's not really a fear of God but rather, the ego's fear of losing control and being displaced in favour of God. Humility opens the door to receiving this power and grace without being burned in the process. Once the ego has been removed from its self-created throne (and pride will keep it in place), the experience of God can enter, giving rise to great joy, peace, and gratitude within.

Chapter 9
Floods and Desire

Tara Protection against Floods

Allhallows, England

Thursday 22 June 2006

This third Tara protects from all water-related disasters and the suffering and sickness arising from the negative aspect of desire and attachment. She is red in colour and holds a fire crystal in the lotus flower in her left hand.

I don't know whether this will be the case for each of the Taras, but there has been a definite transition period between the second and third ones—a period where the energy that built up around one dissolves to make way for the energy arising around the next one.

We are now in the Water element, which has a very different feeling about it. Whereas the Earth element represented the stability and relative solidity of the physical earth, the Water element is much less fixed. It is fluid, malleable, and adaptable; it's regarded as the "bearer of life", as it transports and carries.

It is strongly connected to our emotions. Within the Buddhist understanding, the emotion of desire is the reason we are born into the human realm. The deep-rooted desire to exist, to be a particular "self", is what produces the causes and conditions to manifest in a human body. So, in the quest for enlightenment, freeing ourselves from the negative aspects of desire must be seen as of central importance.

This is perhaps why renunciation is so often advocated and indeed demanded by many spiritual traditions. The mind is so gripped by habitual desire, which is fundamentally a desire for happiness and pleasure, that it runs after all manner of things in the mistaken belief that our happiness, or at least relief from craving, lies in the fulfilment of these desires. Most of us know from bitter experience that this just isn't the case. Renunciation is not meant to be a punishment but rather, a way to steer the mind towards what will truly satisfy desire and give rise to a more lasting peace of mind and happiness.

True renunciation is rather different from that imposed by external authority. The latter can often create problems; resentment, suppression, and denial are all possible consequences of renouncing something in a superficial, premature, or forced way. Swiss psychoanalyst Carl Jung believed that it was not possible to truly renounce anything until it had been fully embraced. In other words, we have to fully experience and allow something to become part of us, or at least so thoroughly examine it that any potential fascination is exhausted. Then renunciation can come quite naturally, like an old skin falling away. No struggle—an effortless letting go.

The emphasis on renunciation varies across different religious traditions. In Buddhism, it is most strongly seen in the Theravadin tradition, where a monk or nun renounces the world completely and lives a simple life where begging for alms is an everyday practice. Within the Vajrayana tradition, renunciation is very much a part of the monastic commitment, but there is a strong emphasis on fully allowing and opening up to whatever arises within the mind, with a view to transforming, or seeing through, the mind's distortions using the tools and practice of various methods.

In this way, nothing need be rejected or pushed away, and all experience can be brought to the spiritual path and used to speed the process of realization. With this view, desire is therefore not a particular problem. Acting on it, however, might be, so the idea is to work skilfully with whatever arises in the mind; getting to know the nature of desire and attachment, for example, and staying relaxed and nonreactive—and perhaps praying to channel the energy or desire into the ultimate desire for enlightenment!

Sunday 25 June 2006

Heading South

I leave Edinburgh tomorrow for good, and that's quite an emotional wrench—parting company from dear friends, giving up the place that has been home for a few years now, really. The city is always here to come back to, but that doesn't have much impact on the nature of a journey such as this, which involves stepping out into the unknown.

Tomorrow, I'm heading down to Samye Ling for the last days of something called a Drupchen and for a meeting with Akong Rinpoche. A Drupchen is a very intense practice. Prayers are done for 24 hours over a period of time, in this case seven days.

It's the first time in the history of Samye Ling that such an event has taken place, and it is said to be a powerful practice for removing obstacles and negativity. Many teachers have been flown over from Sherab Ling in India to do this practice, and it will probably be quite a spectacle—lots of ritual, colourful clothing, and music. This particular Drupchen focuses on Guru Rinpoche, the great Indian yogi responsible for introducing Buddhism to Tibet in the 8th century.

Thursday 29 June 2006
Samye Ling

It's been a very good and inevitably rather intense few days. The energy during such an event is powerful, and rather like entering a completely different reality. Today is the last day of the Guru Rinpoche Drupchen, and I do feel quite transformed and blessed by the whole experience, recognizing the immaculate timing. I was definitely in the right place at the right time.

Two days ago, all of us who were present in the Temple received a special blessing. Akong Rinpoche handed out a small relic of Guru Rinpoche to whoever was there. No one knew what was happening or had been planned, and Rinpoche clearly had complete trust that whoever was there was meant to be in the Temple that morning.

The story behind this event is really rather incredible. During the time of Guru Rinpoche's teaching in Tibet in the 8th century, many treasure texts (*termas*) were hidden, to be revealed hundreds of years later, during a period when they would be of benefit. Such termas are found or revealed by Tertons, or Treasure Revealers.

Guru Rinpoche foresaw the need for genuine relics to inspire devotion and faith and left instructions for multiplying existing ones. This involved blending the relics with elixirs and pressing them into special moulds of different sizes—the substances used coming from a variety of sources deemed auspicious and holy, such as special pills, fragments of brocade, and Guru Rinpoche's hair.

It was widely believed that these moulds had been lost during the Cultural Revolution, but this year—in a seemingly effortless way—one of them was handed to Akong Rinpoche. A Tibetan seer had had a vision of Guru Rinpoche whilst on retreat and had been told that this was now the time to place many consecrated images in various countries. These images would help restore the balance of beings and their environment and combat diseases of the mind and body.

The person who was to carry out this work had a name that began with an "A". A number of signs had led the seer to believe that this person was Akong Rinpoche, and for this reason, Akong Rinpoche had been given one of the moulds. He had then felt inspired to organize and host the Guru Rinpoche Drupchen, inviting some of the most highly regarded masters from Tibet and India to attend and help lead the prayers.

So the relics we were given are very precious. Those of us there that day all have a responsibility to remember Guru Rinpoche's wish and vision. We are to encourage the spread of such positive energy in any way we can, particularly through the building of stupas, temples, or statues, where the images of Guru Rinpoche, said to be living emanations of his mindstream, can be placed.

I was personally very struck by this, in the light of this journey to place images of Tara in different countries, wherever her particular activity and blessing might be of benefit. The similarity was surely not a coincidence. I felt empowered by Guru Rinpoche as a consequence, and deeply grateful for the many blessings that were lighting my way, like lamps in the darkness.

Saturday 8 July 2006

London

I reached London this morning, after a meandering journey down through Yorkshire, Manchester, Leamington, and Oxford. I'm now in West Hampstead. It's good to be back, but the first feelings have been sadness, and tears have flowed as photographs of my father in my brother's flat here remind me that he's gone.

This is the first time I've been back since he died, and the last time I saw him was here. I remember looking at him as he sat in the armchair, wondering if I would see him again. Dad didn't really engage with the reality of his dying, which helped in some ways, because it allowed us all to be in the present moment and live the life that was manifesting there and then. But it didn't make conversation very easy, and I always felt we were avoiding the subject of what was actually going on, because the feelings around it were frightening and difficult.

Relationships with parents are deep, and the connection strong. Coming back into the "stream" of family is usually an emotional time for me. It's a time I can dread, not because there is anything fundamentally wrong with anyone—I have a good family—but because of the conflict within myself: between belonging and not belonging, between loving them and being driven mad by them, and between wanting to stay and be with everyone and needing to leave and go my own way.

* * *

Buddhists regard being born into the human realm as a blessed rebirth, because there is the opportunity to make real progress in terms of understanding the true nature of mind and reality. In some of the other realms, such as the initially very attractive God Realm, it is said that everything is so wonderful there is no motivation to change. Eventually, however, the karma for such an experience is exhausted, and we fall to lower realms. The shock can be unpleasant, and there are no resources to cope with this. So, although the human realm is full of suffering, it acts as a spur to make the kinds of changes that bring about the end of illusion and the dawning of enlightenment.

Suffering, therefore, is good! Or rather, it is inevitable, and from a spiritual point of view, can trigger a willingness to turn away from the traps, temptations, and empty pleasures of worldly life.

Many people feel religions are negative and breed a kind of miserable, bitter self-denial. I don't see it like this. There is nothing wrong with worldly life; it's just that it doesn't offer us anything of any substance at the end of the day, if it is pursued for itself alone. We are not ultimately worldly beings; we are spiritual beings living a worldly existence. Our suffering comes from not understanding this.

It's often said that the Truth is too much for us to bear—the light is too bright. Buddhism tells us that when we die, we have an experience of this light. If we are able to recognize this light as our own minds, then we are liberated on the spot and the compulsory cycle of birth and death ends. But most of us are afraid when we see this light, becoming unconscious or turning away, usually finding ourselves caught once again in the winds of karma, destined to take rebirth somewhere.

* * *

I had a strange experience last week in the Drupchen at Samye Ling that made me think of this teaching. It was whilst I was in the Guru Rinpoche empowerment. I'd gone up to the Vajra Master leading the initiation for a blessing, after which we all moved along a line of lamas who were holding different sacred objects.

We were blessed by each object as we passed, but one of the lamas seemed to make the sign of the cross above my head before pouring *amrita* into my hand. I was so shocked that suddenly everything in my mind stopped, and there was an experience of incredible light. I was pretty freaked out and felt somewhat overwhelmed by it—obliterated in a way.

Later, I realized that perhaps I had been given a glimpse of the great light that is the light of liberation, and, like most people, I was not prepared for it, not able to take advantage of this experience, and so fell back into ordinary perception. A big opportunity missed! Disappointing, but also very useful to see how hard it really is to get beyond the mind that grasps so strongly at its own reality. This is perhaps why spiritual traditions encourage us to train our minds, to prepare ourselves for these moments of unexpected liberation, so that one day we really can merge with the light and go beyond the illusion and limitations of ordinary mind.

Wednesday 12 July 2006

Water Element

I've reached the south of England, and I'm close to the area where the third Tara will be placed. It's clear that water-related problems affect many places and the imbalance of the water element endangers life more than other elements do. But it's also clear that all the elements are interrelated, and whilst one element may manifest in an extreme way—through floods, monsoons, and tsunamis—it is the imbalance in the relationship between the elements that is often the underlying source of the problems that occur.

* * *

With respect to water, it seems that the balance between the life-sustaining and life-threatening qualities of water is particularly delicate. Many people choose to live in and around water: in fact, over half of the world's population lives by the sea, on rivers, or close to water. Not only does this traditionally provide for domestic water consumption but it has also been one of the main ways in which goods are transported and economies trade with each other.

Many civilizations have grown up around rivers and low-lying deltas; for example, Egypt, China, and Bangladesh are all parts of the world that depend heavily on rivers but are frequently at the mercy of their unpredictable behaviour.

In 1988, 62 percent of the land in Bangladesh was underwater after the rivers Brahmaputra and Ganges burst their banks, pouring through villages, uprooting millions of people, and killing over 2,000. In 2005, heavy rains and flood water from India and Nepal caused some of the worst flooding in Bangladesh.

In China, the problem is even worse. Billions of people live along the Yangtze and Yellow rivers, and flooding is common and often severe. So bad is it for the peasants living along the Yellow River, it is known as China's Sorrow. Regular flooding of the land generates very fertile soil, which is one of the great attractions of such areas, but the price to pay during monsoon times is often enormous. In 1991, the Yangtze River flooded an area nearly the size of Britain, killing thousands and making over one million people homeless.

Apart from such obvious devastation, flooding brings other problems, in particular, disease. Without fresh water supplies and with sewage systems ruptured, contaminated water becomes a real source of danger. Many more people die from the complications associated with floods than they do from the floods themselves.

For those of us living in the Western world, floods have undoubtedly been a feature of life, and increasingly so, but rarely on the scale of such countries as Egypt and in the East. But the rising sea levels from the impact of global warming and melting ice caps present many challenges. In Britain, the area under greatest threat is the east and southeast of England, which is already slowly sinking into the sea, but which would suffer huge losses of land if sea levels were to rise even a little. Parts of Norfolk, Sussex, Essex, and Kent are especially vulnerable, and as the North Sea flows into the River Thames, even London could be at risk.

The River Thames has a long and colourful history and passes through some of the most beautiful towns and countryside in the southeast. It's a river that I know very well and have lived beside much of my life. It seems poignant to have chosen this part of the world, and this river in particular, for the placing of the third Tara.

Monday 17 July 2006

River Thames

Travelling by boat along the River Thames on a gentle summer's day, it's easy to be lulled into a false sense of security about this river, or any river. There are dark depths and murky pasts concealed beneath rippling, dappling waters.

In the 18th century, the Thames was one of the busiest waterways in the world, putting London at the centre of the huge mercantile British Empire. It was during this time, however, that one of the worst river disasters in England took place when, in 1878, a crowded pleasure boat collided with another boat, killing 640 people.

Before that, in what became known as the Great Stink of 1858, sittings at the House of Commons and Westminster were abandoned due to the appalling stench coming from the polluted river waters. This incident propelled the city into a major engineering programme to tackle the sewage problem, and giant sewers were constructed on both sides of the embankment under the supervision of Joseph Bazalgette.

We think of the Thames as a dirty river today, but in fact it is relatively clean. Or at least it had been considered so until the more recent practice of water companies dumping sewage in our rivers. However, the tremendous hammering the river took when London was a major world port is over. Rail and road transportation have largely taken the place of river travel, and even the Old Port of London has been moved downstream, out of the heart of the city to Tilbury.

Flooding has always been a feature of life on the Thames, but it wasn't until 1953, when over 300 people were drowned in the city's worst ever flood, that London set about trying to keep the water levels stable. Whilst most of the damage was to the estuary area, around Canvey Island, the absence of any recognizable flood defences at the time put London suddenly on red alert. In 1974, work began on what has become the world's largest movable flood defence: the Thames Barrier. It took 10 years to complete and cost over £500 million, but it is a magnificent feat of water engineering and has been described as the Eighth Wonder of the World.

I took a boat out from Greenwich to see it for myself. Leaving Greenwich, we chugged past the Royal Naval College, now home to Trinity College of Music, then the infamous Millenium Dome, London Docklands, and finally the Barrier itself. Nine great concrete piers stretch across the river, each one buried 50 feet below river level on solid chalk foundations, some weighing 1500 tons. It takes 40 minutes to turn the wheels to raise or lower the floodwall at any given time. The Thames is most at risk from flooding due to tidal surges that happen out in the North Sea; these occasionally find their way into the estuary and result in a sudden rise in water level. It's clear that the Thames Barrier has provided very good protection in recent years, but further defences are going to be needed for the future as rising sea levels threaten the capacity of existing ones.

Thursday 3 August 2006

Allhallows

In a bleak, obscure part of the country, where nothing much happens and the land is flat and mostly given over to grazing and a residential caravan park, I have placed the third Tara. She sits now at Allhallows, on the northern shores of Kent, the official point at which the River Thames ceases and becomes the English Channel, and vice versa.

The Thames Estuary is bigger than I expected and, with the tide out, the mudflats seem to extend for several hundred metres before water can even be seen. On one side is Southend-on-Sea in Essex, then the Isle of Sheppey just beyond Allhallows. It's an unprepossessing place, yet there is a strange peace here.

Walking over the marshland, which is very dry in this drought, and up to the seawall, the wind blew and the cows quietly grazed. Over the seawall, sitting at the edge of the tide, monotones of grey stretched in all directions—pebbled beach, rocks, river, sea, and clouds—confounding the senses and calming the mind.

I sat for quite some time thinking of the Tara journey and the people, places, and events being woven into this pilgrimage. Placing the Tara in a rocky crevice, overlooking the river and the sea, I doubt she'll ever be found. May her blessing spread throughout this corner of England and beyond, protecting all who live in areas where water can adversely affect lives and livelihoods.

* * *

Returning to London, I stopped in Rochester for lunch and to visit the cathedral, the second oldest in the country. It's a beautiful, inspiring building and boasts Britain's finest example of an original medieval wall painting. Painted in the 13th century, the Wheel of Fortune is a metaphor for time and the turning world, with its twists of fate, its uncertainties, and illusory pleasures. I was struck by the similarities between this English depiction of life and the Buddhist Wheel of Fortune, showing the Six Realms of Samsara.

I was also struck by the strong presence of the Holy Mother, both in the Lady Chapel and in the gardens, where there is a modern sculpture of Mary and Jesus commissioned to commemorate the 800th anniversary of the cathedral. In Rochester Cathedral, I was reminded once again of the similarities between Tara and Mary. The Divine Mother has many faces; she is there in so many different ways; we just have to know where and how to look, and follow our hearts.

Chapter 10
Fire and Anger

Tara Protection against Fire

Blackheath, England

Thursday 10 August 2006

I began working with this Tara last week and have no idea where she's going to take me. Australia, California, the Mediterranean, and India are all countries where fires can be a major problem. I'm drawn to Australia, where bushfires are a regular problem, but the commitment to get there is financially prohibitive.

In the meantime, I've been looking at the mind poison of anger and can see how many problems this causes. Just watch the Israelis and Hezbollah launching attack after attack on each other, each side angry with the other and determined to defend itself from the other as the enemy. This is a clear example of what can happen when anger escalates and of the mindset anger gives rise to.

Anger needs an enemy, a belief in separation and irreconcilable difference. It is a fire within the mind, and if it isn't pacified, it can quickly get out of control and inflict a great deal of harm. One of the other problems with anger is that it tends to justify its actions, finding reasons and explanations for itself, and this can make anger very difficult to defuse.

If I look at my own mind, I can see that for many years my mind was disturbed by fairly frequent experiences of anger. There was always a rush of power that came with the anger, and this power kicked words or actions into motion, which seemed to protect me at the time. They certainly removed me from the person or situation that was triggering the anger, but often there was regret afterwards and the realization that I had lost a great deal in the process. It took a long time to realize that anger wasn't a skilful response, and that I needed to work on this within my own mind and not keep blaming others for whatever had upset me.

Within Buddhism, all the poisons have their corresponding wisdom: in other words, emotions are not a problem if we can catch them before they take over. Through mind training, we learn to recognize the essence of our emotions, and this has a naturally liberating effect, releasing the mind from the grip of that particular emotion.

The essence of pure anger, for example, is mirror-like wisdom: a clear, sharp quality in the mind that reflects like a mirror. Maybe you know the experience of the mind suddenly becoming very clear when you're angry. I think that's the mirror-like wisdom dawning, but the secret is to have this clarity without any negative emotion whatsoever. This is very difficult!

I remember hearing that the Dalai Lama still admits he has to work on transforming anger and that, even for him, this is still a vulnerable area. He has good reasons to be angry, and yet his message is consistently one of nonviolence and non-retaliation.

Meeting unprovoked and unjustified violence from others must be one of the toughest challenges on the spiritual path. Jesus also faced this one, and his words from the Cross—"Forgive them, Father, for they know not what they do"—are some of the most powerful words ever spoken, to my mind. Jesus's compassion was so deep and his understanding so complete that he knew that the actions of his "enemies" would only lead to suffering on their part. He knew that whatever suffering he endured at their hands was temporary and transient, but that theirs was likely to get increasingly intense and painful, due to the power of their ignorance and hatred.

Living like Jesus, Gandhi, or the Dalai Lama is not exactly easy, but they provide shining examples of the power of transforming anger into compassion and violence into nonviolence and teach us that this is the only real way to achieve peace in our own minds and in our world.

Thursday 17 August 2006
Conflict

Perhaps not surprisingly, and maybe rather usefully, I have been experiencing a lot of anger this week. I dare say that evoking the presence of this fourth Tara has brought this to consciousness so that I can learn how to transform it.

The predominant reason for these feelings has been conflict about the pilgrimage. Having intended to head off to various parts of the world on my own, I have found that the cost and stress of travel is getting in the way. I've also been sleeping in a room where the next-door neighbour is rather disturbed and wails loudly at all hours of the night! Outside her window, she has posted big sheets of paper with these words written on them:

All the many hours of other people's time,
and the stress inflicted, these are the only realities!!

So I am kept awake experiencing *her* reality, trying to muster compassion and send it through the walls—but usually only managing to do this after about two hours of silently boiling and inwardly shouting, *Will you just bloody shut up?*

I've been watching my mind get hotter and hotter, tighter and tighter, whenever anger arises. In fact the voice of anger—and the personality that accompanies the voice—are quite distinct. I've been sitting with this, bringing awareness to it, sitting through the painful feelings behind the angry ones, and it's amazing how this practice changes things—how the state of mind eases, opens, releases, and how there is always a solution within the extreme emotion: a solution, an insight, that moves things forward in a constructive way, rather than allows them to go round and round in a destructive one.

The answer that came with regard to the conflict around this pilgrimage was quite unexpected. Instead of seeing myself as a separate person, an isolated unit, trying to climb the equivalent of Everest all by myself, there is another view—which is that I am part of a team, a Tara Team, and I don't have to take all the Taras myself; they can be given to others and taken to different places by those who are sympathetic to and understanding of the task at hand.

That way, not only do the Taras get around the world as planned, going where they might be of benefit, but other people also receive the blessing of Tara's protection whilst they're doing the travelling and become an integral part of a big network of compassion and wisdom flowing out into the world.

What a relief! This solution has lifted a huge weight from my shoulders, opening my mind again. Pressure off. Stress dissipating. Anger transformed into mirror-like wisdom! Well, near enough. Certainly, this project no longer feels so overwhelming or terrifying. Thank you, Tara.

Tuesday 22 August 2006
Under My Nose

Very unexpectedly, the fourth Tara has been placed right under my nose. I came back to Blackheath on Sunday and, whilst doing Tara practice, it became clear that the fourth Tara should go in the garden of my family home. When I thought about this, I realized how appropriate—if a bit shocking—this was. Over the years there's been a lot of anger and many arguments at home, and my own fiery temperament has definitely contributed to this. But this is also a family with a lot of love, and we work hard to understand each other and overcome our problems. The change over the years has been enormous, and the family home has been the crucible through which so much has been worked out.

So, whilst I have been contemplating Australia, Southern California, Spain, or the South of France for this Tara—places where wildfires frequently rage and cause terrible destruction—I have gone no further than my own backyard for her resting place.

More than anything, this has shown me that I cannot predict in advance where Tara is going to take me, and that it isn't me who is in charge of this! I find that liberating and reassuring, which I guess is also the blessing of Tara. I also realize that there is no "working for the benefit of others" that does not directly emerge from the work that I do on myself.

Chapter 11
I Am Not Just "Me"

Tara Protection against Wind Destruction

Greenwich, England

Saturday 19 August 2006

Introducing the fifth Tara. This one protects from dangers related to the Air element—hurricanes, tornadoes, and storms—and from suffering and sickness arising from the negative emotion of jealousy.

When it comes to jealousy, one of the most insidious of the mind poisons, this truly is a "green-eyed monster" at its most intense. Like many people, I've experienced jealousy which, when examined closely, always seems to have something to do with abandonment, loss, or lack, and the sense of incompletion—wanting something that someone else has and hurting inside because of the belief that it's not possible for oneself.

As with all the mind poisons, it's possible to transform jealousy, and jealousy (or envy) already has within it a corresponding wisdom, according to the Buddhist view. It is described as "all accomplishing wisdom", and I've often struggled to understand what is really meant by that.

As far as my current understanding goes, I see it like this. When our minds are free from jealousy, we have energy available to accomplish a great deal. Our motivation is strong to accomplish many things, and we believe we can have what we want. There is no sense of lack, either within our minds or the outside world, and we work hard to attain our desires. We are under the influence of "all accomplishing wisdom".

Another way of understanding "all accomplishing wisdom" is to think of the interconnectedness among all beings and remember that we are not truly separate from each other, so one person's joy or success is also our own. Joy is a natural by-product when jealousy is transformed. We celebrate the happiness and success of others. We are happy when good things happen to others and feel included, rather than excluded, in the positive events that happen to them. These are some first thoughts that come up when I think about the nature of this fifth Tara, but we will see what lessons unfold!

Monday 28 August 2006

Empowerments

His Eminence the 18th Dulmo Choje Rinpoche has been in the UK this month. It's the first time he has left his home country of Tibet, and it's rare for someone of his high rank to visit. I have been very fortunate to see him in London, where I took the Bodhisattva Vow with him and received a White Tara empowerment.

An empowerment is a sacred ritual whereby a master with the right qualifications is temporarily transformed into the actual deity—in this case, White Tara—and, through the elaborate ceremony, implants the "seed syllable" (or essence) of the deity within our mind stream. It is also the formal means through which one is authorized to do the *sadhana* practice, which can then allow the qualities of the deity to mature within one's heart and mind. Not every *sadhana* practice requires empowerment, but some do, and this acts as a safeguard to ensure the mind is truly aligned with the deity, and not getting lost in fantasy or useless imagination. The Bodhisattva Vow signifies a commitment taken to work towards enlightenment for the sake of all beings.

I have taken the Bodhisattva Vow before, with Ringu Tulku Rinpoche in a private ceremony, and have not felt the need to take it again. However, this vow is good to take over and over, to keep the mind focused on the sometimes difficult practice of putting others before oneself.

I decided to retake the vow with the group here in London, realizing that it is fundamental to anything we do on a spiritual path, and more important perhaps even than empowerments. Without remembering the importance of others, there are very real dangers we can use the spiritual path as a means to bolster our egos and/or secure our own happiness at the expense of others.

Whether it was the power of the ceremonies and of Dulmo Choje Rinpoche's presence, I don't know, but I felt very weird on Saturday evening. I think my physical system is under a lot of strain—from crazy hormones, bleeding, herbs, and perhaps a lack of iron—and sometimes I don't feel well at all and have very odd symptoms. However, I've decided this is absolutely inseparable from a Tara pilgrimage, and the journey happens to be taking me through the female body right now, rather than around the world.

I have been reflecting on jealousy a little more. I've been aware of seeing friends with babies and feeling curious about why this has never been my reality. I'm 40 now, and the opportunity seems very far away: I have wanted children a great deal, but only if the conditions were right. Sometimes I think I have been jealous about other people having children, but not significantly. I think I just want to be like other women, capable of reproducing and in harmony with that part of my nature and physical make-up. But, as I seem to be entering an early menopause, it seems as if I will never know now whether I could have even conceived a child. It's odd to grieve this, but it seems to be part of what's happening.

A White Tara empowerment is connected to healing and long life. I'm grateful to have received this particular empowerment at this time. It's needed!

Saturday 9 September 2006

Greenwich Park

Today—again unexpectedly—I have placed the fifth Tara, and the Tara Protection against Wind Destruction and Jealousy has gone to Greenwich Park. I have placed her here because of the number of beautiful trees in this park and the devastation that can be caused when storms and strong winds take down these most precious beings.

I have also been battling jealousy on discovering that an old, much-loved boyfriend is getting married. He always loved trees, and in many ways opened my heart and mind to the magic of trees, so it seemed appropriate to offer the fifth Tara to one of the trees in the ancient Royal Park of Greenwich. I had already decided to take some beads from my broken crystal *mala* and offer them to one of the trees in gratitude, when the little Tara statue sitting on my shrine caught my attention and practically jumped into my pocket!

My destination was a beautiful, big, old chestnut tree planted in 1642, one of the oldest trees in the park. I sat meditating with the tree for a while, reflecting on the hundreds of years it's stood there, quietly growing amidst the tumult and changes in London over that time: the Black Death, the Plague, wars, the comings and goings of kings and queens, all the millions of ordinary folk living out their lives in the shadow of this great tree.

Storms, whether meteorological, political, personal, economic, have battered people and places. Trees have fallen, but this one stands today as a testament to the enduring power of nature to withstand it all. I found a deep crevice in the bark of the tree, and tucked Tara inside, praying as I did, for her blessing to be carried on the wind to all who need it.

Tara Increasing Activities

Sydney Botanical Gardens, Australia

Friday 15 September 2006

As I mentioned earlier, there is now a shift taking place in terms of how the pilgrimage will proceed. The ground for this was laid a few weeks ago when the "I am not just me" realization opened the door for others to become an integral part of this journey.

It looks as if the next Taras will be travelling to different parts of the world, but with different people, all of whom have a connection to Tara and whose reason for travelling will be aligned to the specific activity of whichever Tara they are given. My work will be to continue to do the practice with each one in turn and await inspiration and synchronicity with regard to who she is to be given to. I am hoping that each person will also write something about their journey and that this can be included here.

The expansion of the pilgrimage and the project in this way feels appropriate—both liberating and joyful and more inclusive and shared. Interestingly, the lessening of "ownership" within this project, which has been forced on me through recognition of my limits, is a curious feeling. On the one hand, from the point of view of the project and I think the "real me", it's joyful and heart-warming. From the point of view of the ego, it's a bit threatening!

I gratefully stepped into this pilgrimage as some kind of salvation from the devastating losses of the year and the inability to regain control of my life at that point. Mixing ego with spirituality is not ideal, but must be inevitable whilst the ego still has such a hold, consciously or unconsciously. The best one can hope is that consciousness gradually dawns anyway and that the ego is weakened in the process.

So when I woke up this morning with the familiar heart palpitations and anxiety, I looked more directly at what the mind was reacting to. I know these can be symptoms of grief, but who, or what, is experiencing grief?

When I meditated on this question, what I saw was a void, an abyss, a great chasm of nothingness and a feeling of being pulled in. This is what is giving rise to fear. Within the void I can sense clear light, clarity, boundlessness, which is going to obliterate the past that I have been grieving.

Can I let go into that? Can I really trust and surrender to it? It's a precious opportunity to go in and experience it, knowing it is probably the only direction to go in if something new is going to emerge from the ashes of the past. And yet it's really hard to let go of the past, hard to let go even of my suffering! Because it feels like "me" to a large degree and so, there's a real fear of annihilation.

However, even if I can just loosen my sense of identity a little, that is progress. When I was doing my daily Tara practice—a practice that encourages us to see ourselves as the deity rather than an ordinary person—there was definitely a sense of expansion rather than annihilation. I could see that the seemingly separate "I" committed to this Peace Pilgrimage wasn't a separate entity at all.

At the level of Tara herself, there are many beings that are a part of this work, and it doesn't matter who takes the Tara blessing around the world—the more, the merrier, in fact, especially as the connection each person has with Tara on a personal level is strengthened by their willingness to act in this way. This means that Tara's blessing is spreading in more ways than I ever envisaged possible at the beginning of this project.

Tara Increasing Activities is the sixth Tara. She has been given to my mother and stepfather and is now on her way to Australia. Allan is a medical doctor, and he is giving a lecture at a medical conference in Sydney. He will be talking about the research he has been doing for 30 years, looking at the health benefits of vitamin B (thiamine) when given to patients with chronic alcohol problems. There is significant statistical evidence to show that long-term brain damage can be reversed or prevented if this vitamin is administered in the right quantities under the right conditions.

Tara Increasing Activities increases intelligence, eloquence, knowledge, success, wealth, and harmony. It is perfect that she is going to such an event, and also perfect that she is the one to be increasing the global scope of this pilgrimage.

My mother is also going, and she will look after this Tara. I have often felt that my mother is a manifestation of Tara in her own right, so it is fitting that she should be carrying one with her. A keen gardener, she will take her to Sydney's botanical gardens. Given that most medicine is derived from plants, this seems a fitting place.

Tara Enhancing Indestructibility

Seattle, Washington, USA

Monday 18 September 2006

This seventh Tara—Tara Enhancing Indestructibility—has been given to my friend Rob, who is taking her to a new community he will be living in outside Seattle in the US Pacific Northwest. Rob is an architect and former monk at Samye Ling.

Whilst there, he designed and managed the building of The Victory Stupa in the grounds. This was a huge undertaking and took over 10 years to complete, beginning in the 1990s with the consecration of the land.

Stupas are physical structures that are manifestations of enlightened mind, and it is said that anyone who sees or touches one is assured enlightenment—in either this or a future lifetime. They also represent the Buddha in meditation and are what are known as psycho-spiritual structures, spanning the physical, spiritual, and psychological dimensions. It is said that a stupa exists in the invisible world before it exists in physical form, so the first stage of building a stupa is to bring it from the mind and spirit into the physical.

For those involved in the construction of a stupa, there are, therefore, inevitably many significant challenges that will be and need to be faced along the way. In the case of the one at Samye Ling, it involved many fundraising initiatives, including three long treks in the Himalayas in Nepal led by mountaineers Sir Chris Bonnington CBE, Doug Scott CBE, and Hamish McInnes.

In many ways stupas represent indestructibility. Their construction follows strict rules, and the symbolic representation of the Five Elements (Earth, Water, Fire, Air, and Space) is said to bring stability to the environment. They also frequently hold relics of the Buddha and can house the ashes of the deceased.

Curiously, during the period when the Victory Stupa and surrounding Peace Garden were being built, there was a serious accident one December morning, when an unladen logging lorry skidded on black ice and ploughed through the hedge into the newly built Prayer Wheel House surrounding the Stupa. The Prayer Wheel House was completely destroyed, but the Victory Stupa was left undamaged. It was indestructible!

Meeting Rob in London before his trip to Seattle, I realized that he was the appropriate person to carry this particular Tara on her mission. His intention is to take her to the top of one of Washington's highest volcanoes: Mount Rainier in the young Cascade Range outside Seattle. Standing well over 14,000ft above sea level, Mount Rainier—also known as Tahoma, its Native American name—is an active volcano, one of the most dangerous in the United States, since it is close to large population centers. It is topped by glaciers and not an easy climb, but it is fitting that Rob should take this Tara on a "mountain trek" after the Pilgrimage Treks that raised so much of the money needed to build Samye Ling's Victory Stupa.

Tara Protection against Weapons

Moscow, Russia

Wednesday 20 September 2006

Tara Protection against Weapons is dark blue in colour. In Buddhism, the colour blue is often associated with the mind poison of anger and its innate mirror-like wisdom when transmuted. The deities that help us transform our anger are often more wrathful in nature, both through their colour and their physical appearance. Tara Protection against Weapons is one such deity—appropriately so, perhaps.

This eighth Tara was given to my Russian friend Natalya just before she returned home to Moscow. I had met Natalya on Holy Isle and then at Samye Ling and we'd quickly recognised what felt like a strong bond from another life. But whilst I harboured romantic "memories" of Russia, Natalya struggled to accept her heritage. Being part Ukrainian, Tatar, and Chuvash, psychologically she had never felt truly Russian although she had been born there and lived in Russia all her life. She'd spent her earliest years in a little village with her grandmother whilst her parents were in Afghanistan, happy years. But home life in Moscow when her parents returned wasn't happy and she had started looking for a way out. Religious studies at school introduced her to Buddhism, but it was when she met an English monk who was visiting Moscow from Samye Ling that her interest really grew. By her own admission, it was as much the monk as the teachings that drew her but, in sharp contrast to my own experience, Lama Yeshe had warmly invited her to come over to Scotland and to take robes as a novice nun. Natalya and I were kindred spirits, but with very different lives—and karma!

When the time came for Natalya to return to Russia, it was clear she didn't want to go back. I was very sad to say goodbye and although I couldn't go with her, I could give her a little Tara. So, with Tara Protection against Weapons packed safely in her suitcase, Natalya returned to Moscow. She later sent her account of how her journey with this Tara unfolded:

Everything in the Universe has a purpose.
There are no misfits, there are no freaks, there are no accidents.
There are only things we do not understand.

– Marlo Morgan[4]

I woke up 20 minutes before the alarm clock rang. A few days before, I had scheduled to go to the church with my mother so it was quite an early rise. I still could not figure out what woke me at 6 am, but, before falling into a deep sleep, I suddenly came to understand a very profound thing.

I have been a Buddhist practitioner for five years but was born Orthodox. Orthodox Christianity is the predominant religion in Russia. Before I started to become involved in Buddhism, I was not a believer but went to church as much as I could to try to find the answer to the many questions in my heart. But it was Buddhism that helped me to re-evaluate many things about myself and the world. Yet, through my studies in Buddhism, I rediscovered Christianity, and find it a wonderful religion, though it seems to me the main message was misinterpreted and many things distorted.

On this occasion, I returned to Moscow from the UK and brought with me a tiny Tara statue blessed by Akong Rinpoche from Samye Ling in

Scotland, given to me by Anna as part of her Peace Pilgrimage and fund-raising project. The one I have with me is Tara Protecting from Weapons, who is usually pictured as dark blue in colour. I did not have any idea where to place her! I decided to wait and see. To a certain extent, I could not relate to the "weapons" issue. I know that there are always hazards regarding terrorist attacks any time in the world, and there is a difficult situation in the southern part of my country—Chechnya—just now, but something was hampering me, and I was confused and disorientated.

There has been a series of illnesses in my family recently, and my younger brother has been suffering from quite a serious disease, which has unsettled my mother and leaves her constantly on the verge of tears. The last couple of months I haven't felt so good myself, either, and have thought it might have been due to a lack of vitamins and my limited vegetarian diet. I get tired very quickly so have not been doing much since arriving home in Moscow.

One day, my mother's sister paid us a visit and suggested that we might like some spiritual healing; there was an event that was going to happen in the local church. Considering that my parents are non-believers, it was amazing to me that my mother should agree and, throwing a sideways glance at me, said it will be a good idea for us all to go to the Orthodox Church service. I smiled to myself, as they probably thought I would refuse the whole idea point-blank, but I did not want to challenge them and said that I was eager to go, leaving all my Buddhist "antics" for a moment!

And then the night before the service, I finally realized where the tiny Tara Protecting against Weapons should be placed.

It became so clear to me that a weapon needn't just be an actual object but could be figuratively anything we use to fight with. And then I thought about the word, either written or spoken, and how this is our chief means of human communication and relationship.

In the Bible, we read "In the Beginning was the Word . . .", and in our human realm, it becomes a powerful tool to influence each other's lives: to praise, to blame, to accuse, to lie. How much misunderstanding there can be as a result of "the word". Sometimes, the word is used as an expression of love and goodwill, but very often it is used to decry, to condemn, and kill.

I meet a lot of people who are devotees of all sorts of religions, and among the most intolerant are the Orthodox Christians I meet in my own country. Usually intolerance is based on ignorance and simple misunderstanding about the fundamentals of other religions, but most people would not see or be able to understand what lies behind the words. We often think that the word is truth itself, but actually it's only a reflection of it. Sometimes we just do not want to see a bigger picture because it's more comfortable to stay with what's familiar. To accept the fact we might be wrong is frightening, and we often prefer to protect our small egos from "invaders". I'm reminded of a quote from Neale Donald Walsch in his book Conversations with God, *where he speaks of the power of words:*

> Everything you say is a thought expressed. It is creative and sends forth creative energy into the Universe. Words are more dynamic (thus, some might say more creative) than thought, because words are a different level of vibration from thought. They disrupt (change, alter, affect) the Universe with greater impact. Words are the second level of creation.[5]

How powerful words can be! But words still reflect our conceptual thinking, and that is why words are the least reliable purveyor of Truth.

Thinking this way, I wanted to do something that would stand for the idea that the real Truth is unnameable. At the same time, I would like people to be more aware of how they use their words.

I realized that this Tara should be placed near the Orthodox Church, to symbolize a maturing understanding of true spirituality, where words are used for good and not as weapons. After the service, I put little Tara in a hole in the ground by a small fir tree. I pray that we use our words wisely and with kindness and that we be mindful not to willingly harm a living soul with our words.

Tara Protection against Politics

Drolma Lhakang, Tibet

Tuesday 26 September 2006

This ninth Tara Protection against Politics is sometimes referred to as Tara Protecting from Political Oppression. Throughout the world, we can see just how much political oppression there is and how difficult it can be to resist. Standing up to the worst kind of oppression can cost you your freedom, your rights, even your life and it is sometimes, often, easier just to accept it and try to make the best of one's experience.

These are the very obvious, external realities of politically oppressive systems, but what about the internal nature of political oppression? How often do we suppress our emotions, our desires, our instincts in order to comply with the authority of an inner voice that seeks to control us? That inner voice may once have been an outer one—a parent, teacher, someone in a position of authority—but the influence of such voices conditions young impressionable minds and the two can become virtually indistinguishable.

When it comes to Tara's protection from oppression, once again it is how she helps to protect our mind that matters most. What better than to remember the eternal freedom that lies at the core of our being, no matter the external circumstances? Tara can help us do this and in so doing, remind us that nothing and no one can truly oppress us. We are, and always have been, free.

And yet, on a more mundane, everyday level, there is enormous suffering inflicted on people, animals, land through the brutal actions of dictators around the world. And this ninth Tara is needed in so many places. It has become very clear in recent days, however, where this particular one wants to go.

My friend Sara was going on a three-week pilgrimage to Tibet and, with her own strong and active commitment to peace and alleviating suffering in the world, was very much the right person for this particular mission. She does a lot of work with Amnesty International, and the suffering of people oppressed by political regimes is very close to her heart. She also lives in Findhorn much of the time, and the pilgrimage was being organized and led by the aptly named Thomas Warrior from the Shambhala Retreat Centre in the nearby village of Forres.

This is her account of working with this Tara:

Tara arrived beautifully wrapped, and I placed the small package on my shrine. I positioned her with care amongst my belongings and prayed that my inner guidance would let me know where I should place her. On our pilgrimage, we were going to visit a number of different sacred sites in and around Lhasa.

When we landed at the airport, the sight of the Chinese guards was an immediate reminder of the political realities of Tibet. I placed my Tara in my hand. The bus sped along the road, and outside we had our first glimpse of this extraordinary country.

The mountainous landscape was barren but spectacular. Alongside, we could see the broad stretches of the Brahmaputra River, which has its source at Mt. Kailash, Tibet's most sacred mountain. We drove along a modern highway. To their credit, the Chinese are good at building roads; however, the natural protection afforded Tibet through its inaccessibility and remoteness is now being seriously undermined.

We soon drew up outside a very ancient temple called Drolma Lhakang. This temple was originally built by Atisha, the great Indian Mahasiddha who did so much for Mahayana and Vajrayana Buddhism, and it is dedicated to Tara. Atisha had a special connection with Tara, having had a dream as a young man in which she appeared, telling him not to get too attached to worldly pleasures.

Drolma Lhakang was my first glimpse of these extraordinary ancient Tibetan buildings and of golden prayer wheels and prayer flags fluttering high above in the breeze. Overhead the sky was vivid blue. Our guide, Thomas Warrior, invited us to open ourselves to feel the energies of this very special place, which remarkably was one of the few monasteries left intact. It was here that we invoked Tara's blessing for our pilgrimage.

Inside the temple, it was extraordinary to see, in the middle chamber, a shrine dedicated to the 21 Taras, and in the centre of this—behind a thick grille and therefore scarcely visible—was the original Tara made by Atisha. Viewing this left me with feelings of awe and reverence. The significance of this precious place being left intact, despite the maelstrom that affected the rest of the country, inescapably links it to Tara's blessing and protection.

I immediately felt that this was the right place for my own Tara. My only hesitation was that we had only just arrived and had several other important temples to visit. I consulted with Thomas, and he immediately said that this was the right place. I was intrigued by the suddenness and quickness of all of this as these are also qualities associated with Tara. She responds immediately!

I placed her with great care underneath the main Tara, along with a khata *(a traditional white ceremonial scarf), which I had brought with me from Kopan Monastery in Nepal, where we began.*

At Kopan this morning, some of us had spoken to one of the monks, who told us that he was from Shigatze in Tibet. His parents had fled to safety in Nepal when he was a small boy. He spoke wistfully of his homeland and asked us to bring him back a piece of Tibet when we returned at the end of our pilgrimage. I was struck by the extraordinary injustice of us being able to board a plane and arrive here, whereas he, a Tibetan, is still in exile and cannot return home.

I thought of him and of so many others whose situation is similar, most notably his Holiness the Dalai Lama. I thought of Tara and imagined the deep floodwaters of her compassion going out to the Tibetan people, who have suffered so much through the catastrophe of the Chinese occupation. I also imagined her compassion flowing out to the Chinese. What strange karma has brought them here, and is there some deeper significance within all that has happened?

My prayer as I placed Tara was that this time of oppression swiftly come to an end, and that HH the Dalai Lama be able to return to make an active contribution to the healing of his people.

It was then time to continue our journey. The rest of our pilgrimage was equally moving, and we were able to visit several wonderful places. We did on a couple of different occasions, however, experience problems that could have seriously affected our visit. On these occasions, Thomas encouraged us to recite Tara's mantra. I felt sure that through doing this we were able to invoke her protection—and certainly each time we did, the threatened disruption was averted.

So my gratitude is immense for having been able to participate in this project, which I hope will bring Tara's blessing to many different situations. It felt particularly special to have been invited to take her to her homeland at this present time, when the political situation in Tibet remains as intractable as ever and, therefore, the faith people have in Tara, the Mother of all Buddhas, is of inestimable importance.

What Sara didn't know at the time was that Drolma Lhakang is also Akong Rinpoche's monastery in Tibet. It is extraordinary that she should have gone all that way with a Tara in her pocket blessed by him and placed her under the most sacred Tara in his monastery without realizing the connection. Truly, this is the power of Tara!

Tara Protection against Thief

Goa, India

Friday 29 September 2006

The 10th Tara, Tara Protection against Thief, has been given to friends, who are taking their twin daughters, Tara and India, for a five-month stay in Goa in Southern India.

Originally close friends of my brother, I got to know Justin and Lizzy much better when they were expecting the twins and Lizzy was experiencing difficulties in her pregnancy. I had only met Lizzy once, but I had a very strong experience around the time I heard about these problems and how worried she was about what was happening, or what might happen.

I woke up one morning with a strong urge to get in touch with her—so strong that, despite fearing I might be invading her privacy as a relative stranger, I took up the pen and wrote what I hoped would be a supportive letter. I wrote about Tara and her capacity to protect from fear and danger. I prayed at the same time that Tara would be with her.

It wasn't until after the twins were born that I heard further news. All had gone well. I was overjoyed that all three of them, mother and daughters, were safe and well. It was then that I also learnt that Justin and Lizzy had decided to call one of the twins Tara!

So, it was wonderful to discover their intended journey and wholly appropriate that they be given the next Tara. It wasn't obvious why it should be the Tara Protection against Thief, though India is of course famous for pickpockets! But perhaps it was to do with the fact that their daughters were nearly "stolen" from them before they were born. Whatever the reason, I never questioned the guidance and synchronicity around each Tara and who she was meant to be given to.

Several months later, Justin sent a message from Goa, and in that time, the deeper significance of why this particular Tara went with them was revealed:

In South Goa, there is a beach with a rocky promontory on its north side. The rocks look out on the fishermen in the bay. The fishermen look out on tourists. The beach is called Patnam.

For seven months of the year, Patnam is a resort. Cooks and waiters commute from northern India and Nepal and Bangladesh. The sun shines, music seeps from stereos, and tourists sip cold beers in bamboo shacks and watch their tattoos redden. There is no rain; wind whispering through palm trees giving only the illusion of rain. There are no clouds. Every evening the fishermen cross the bay in boats of mango wood, black and tar-stained and weighed down with Western flesh. There are no fish anymore. Industrial trawlers on the horizon have drained the seas. The tourists sit in their boats and admire the sunset. The fishermen take their money and dream of being somewhere else.

And then the season ends.

For five months of the year there is no tourism, no money; there is the monsoon, dark clouds, and strong winds and rain. The sea rises, boils, beats upon the shore, and the fishermen take their boats beyond the bay. Only now, when the trawlers retire to harbour and wait out the storms, do the fish return. And so the fishermen take out their boats and cast their nets, and every year a few fail to return—lives stolen by the wind and the rain and the sea.

In South Goa there is a beach with a rocky promontory on its north side. The rocks look out on fishermen in the bay. Amidst these rocks there is now a Tara. Perhaps the sea will be kinder this year.

I was very touched by Justin's story about the fishermen in Patnam and how he'd tucked the little Tara into the rocks overlooking the sea, intending that her presence there bring kindness to these fishermen.

I was reminded once again of the deep interdependence between all living beings and the planet that we call home. That when we take more than we really need from any natural source, we are very likely to be stealing from one of our fellow sentient beings, perhaps endangering their very life. Indigenous people, people who live close to Nature in all her wild and beautiful forms, understand and respect this relationship far better than those who have become urbanized and disconnected from the natural environment.

On the inner level, Tara Protection against Thief is said to guard us from wrong views. Wrong views can lead us into great danger, and modern society seems to have strayed so far and so blindly from the original ways that we are facing the very real possibility of a mass extinction event. We are wise to honour the ways of folk who live and die in the untamed embrace of a sea where Neptune's trident might one day fish for them too.

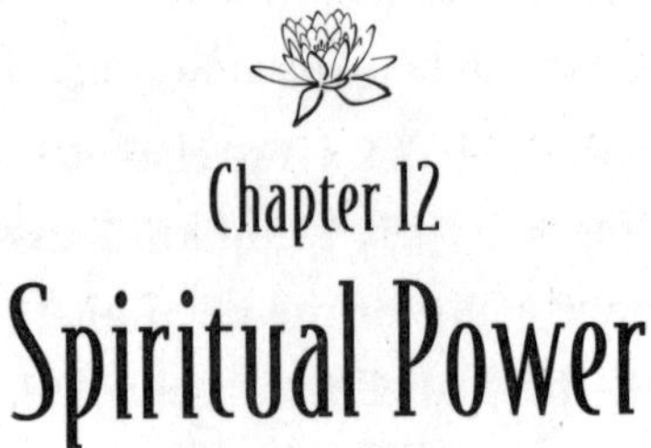

Chapter 12
Spiritual Power

Tara Increasing Power

Amma

Monday 2 October 2006

Gurus

After sending the 10th Tara to India, I found myself thinking about the quintessential Indian tradition of gurus. Gurus are also very important within the Tibetan Buddhist tradition, and I am wondering about their relationship with the deities.

Guru literally means "dispeller of darkness". Whether that's the darkness of ignorance or the darkness of suffering, it doesn't matter;

they are inseparably linked. I'm in Oxford this week, staying with an older, close friend, and someone who has played a big role in my spiritual life, as she taught me to meditate in my early 20s.

Also here this week, visiting from India, is one of the teachers from my lineage in Buddhism: Khenchen Thrangu Rinpoche, a senior teacher within the Kagyu lineage and the main teacher for the four regents of this lineage, including His Holiness the 17th Karmapa. I have never seen him and am looking forward to being reminded of the benefits of a meditation practice, the subject I understand he is to teach!

Meanwhile, I've been reading the biography of one of India's most celebrated saints, Sri Ramana Maharshi. This is having quite an impact.

Ramana was born in South India in the late 1800s and, at a very young age, left home and took himself off to live an austere and intense life of silence, meditation, and solitude within the halls of a local temple. He renounced the world completely, shaving his hair, giving away the last of his very little money, and donning a loincloth in place of clothing. He ate very little and ignored all attempts to be lured into conversation—he just sat and sat, moving occasionally if need be, but otherwise totally absorbed in meditation and unaware of the world around him.

He was eventually drawn to the mountain of Arunachala, considered to be a holy place by the Hindus, the abode of Shiva, God of Light. There, he remained for the rest of his life, gradually shedding the last remnants of his identity as an ordinary person and becoming, if such a person can really be described at all, a fully embodied Divine Being, fully enlightened. He seemed "extraordinarily ordinary" at first glance, and yet so powerful that the energy emanating from him drew people from all over the world, who just came to be close to him. They wanted to receive his grace, which was regarded as none other than the grace of God.

His teaching was very simple. He did not profess to belong to any religion, but thought all religions lead to the same place: the experience of Oneness, where any vestige of ego was left behind and the mind absorbed into its very source—*advaita*, or non-duality. Here, there is total silence, but not the silence of no noise, but rather the silence of no thought.

Reading his biography, I am reminded of an experience I once had in my house in Woodstock. It was not long after my friend and client Ann had died, and I had been contemplating death and dying a great deal.

On one such occasion, I recall that all of a sudden, every noise stopped dead, and there was complete silence—but this was not external silence; it was internal. I remember asking the question, "Why have all the birds stopped singing?" before everything went kind of blank—but not a vacant blank; it was more of a buzzing, alive blank. Pure peace, absolute nothingness. It was heaven!

Then came a roaring sound and the word *advaita* appeared in my consciousness at the same time as this sense of pure nothingness began "falling" and fragmenting into discrete entities of thought, object, and form. I never understood what this was, but perhaps it was a glimpse of the Absolute.

Sri Ramana taught through silence. He gave very little actual teaching, except that he would ask students (or devotees, as they were usually called) to contemplate the question "Who am I?" There is nothing more important than to trace this "I" back to its source, and there to lose it! The "I" thought is the thought preceding all other thoughts, and is therefore the root of the human condition. To transcend our human condition, with all its attendant confusion and suffering, is to experience the Truth of who we really are and to know Heaven on Earth. Sri Ramana regarded this as the only teaching worth having. He also believed that at a certain point in our development, it is necessary to be with a guru, in order to be able to reach realization.

Reading this book has stirred the same realization within me. I have often felt it and am very grateful to Akong Rinpoche, Ringu

Tulku Rinpoche, and Lama Yeshe, who all fulfil that role for me. But there are times when the longing becomes very intense, such as it is now. Perhaps that's because I'm not physically close to any of them right now, but also because I've lost my father and feel the need for something or someone to fill that void. It's said that "When the student is ready, the teacher will appear."

So, how does this relate to Tara? Does it relate? I've heard it said that the deity is also the guru, but it can be hard to have such a strong, clear connection with the deity: They are not in form and only visible within the mind's eye, which is obviously subject to all sorts of interference and interpretation by the conceptual mind. A guru can be a deity in form, however, as they can manifest in any form, depending on what will be of benefit. So I'm curious. Gurus are in my awareness at the moment, as I begin to work with Tara Increasing Power.

Saturday 7 October 2006

Thrangu Rinpoche

I feel very fortunate to be able to go to see Thrangu Rinpoche who is teaching in Oxford just now. The teaching I attended was on The Four Thoughts, the thoughts that turn the mind to the Dharma. Basically they remind us of why it is important to practise the Dharma.

The Four Thoughts are 1) precious human birth; 2) death and impermanence; 3) karma, cause and effect; and 4) the problems of *samsara*.

We were reminded of how fortunate we are to have this precious human birth. Apparently, it is very rare to be born into a body and mind that are relatively healthy and able to listen to and understand the teachings—even more fortunate to have the connection with the Dharma and be able to receive these teachings directly.

Once we realize how lucky we actually are to have this human life, we need to know how best to use it. This is where the following three thoughts can help us. When we meditate on death and impermanence, it can be a bit depressing because we really face up to the reality of what this ordinary life is about. Everything changes. Everything that comes into form will eventually decay and die. Every type of worldly happiness is subject to change and usually won't last very long.

When we look at the many things that happen to us, we wonder what it is that is the cause of good or bad fortune. We wonder what makes things happen in the way they do. The teaching on karma, cause and effect states quite simply that every thought, word, and action has a consequence—either immediately or in the future. So if our minds are polluted with many negative thoughts and feelings, we are likely to be acting in negative ways as a result, and creating unhappiness for ourselves or others now or in the future. If our minds can be purified, if we can develop the positive qualities within the mind and diminish the negative ones, then we will be creating the causes for happiness.

Often, however, we attribute happiness to the wrong thing. We believe that happiness is dependent on, and caused by, certain external things, such as money, physical appearance, relationships, status, fame, possessions, and so forth. So we spend a lot of time and effort chasing these and then trying to hold onto them, failing to realize that not only will they not last but they probably won't bring us that much happiness, anyway. These are the problems of *samsara*, the cycle of birth and death to which life in the material world is bound.

Reflecting and meditating on these Four Thoughts gives us the motivation to turn our minds towards something that will really bring us happiness—in the short term, in the long term, and ultimately, a state of permanent, stable happiness unaffected by whatever is happening within or around us.

That something is the Dharma. The Dharma literally means "Truth". It isn't exclusively Buddhist at all, but the path within

Buddhism to realize the Truth is sound and effective and can be relied on.

I have reflected and meditated on these teachings and felt very inspired by them, so I was sorry to leave Oxford and return to London without seeing Thrangu Rinpoche again. Little did I know that I was about to have another opportunity to see him in London. He was teaching at Samye Dzong, and I had the opportunity to attend this final session before he flew back to India. I could only see this as the blessing of the guru!

Monday 9 October 2006

Amma

I cannot quite believe an opportunity to see another guru has come so quickly! Today I was at Crystal Palace in London, where Amma has arrived from India for her annual visit. Amma—or more formally, Sri Mata Amritanandamayi Devi—is something of a phenomenon in human form. Known as India's "hugging saint", for over 30 years she has travelled around the world, offering comfort, upliftment, and love to millions of people. She works tirelessly and selflessly to bring peace and hope and help transform the suffering of beings everywhere. To me, she is a true embodiment of Tara.

Her *darshan,* her personal blessing, is unique and given in the form of a hug. This is not quite the normal hug you might expect from a loved one; it is much more formal and always involves her whispering the name of the Divine Mother or something sacred in your ear, over and over like a mantra. I arrived in the morning and queued for several hours before I was finally kneeling in front of Amma. I gave her my offering of a flower and was suddenly in her warm embrace, leaning against her shoulder, her white sari smelling of fragrant rose petals; I noticed it was stained slightly with the lipstick and makeup of all the people who had been hugged before me. She whispered words in my ear, but they were in her native tongue of Malayalam, and I didn't know their meaning. But I knew their intention. As a living emanation of the Divine Mother, Amma's sole purpose is to awaken and strengthen this same essence in each and every one of us. This is the purpose of the hug. It is for our healing and wellbeing, but also to empower us to serve and help and love others.

Over the years, Amma has initiated hundreds of charities and charitable activities, from relief work to medical aid, from education centres to orphanages, from research institutes to temples. She has been awarded the Nobel Peace Prize and many other prizes in recognition of her incredible work. She makes it seem and sound so simple: All we have to do is be willing to work selflessly for the benefit of others; not only will this bring huge changes to the lives of others but it will also bring great happiness to us.

I offered Amma the small but powerful 11th Tara—Tara who Increases Power. She does not perhaps need this Tara for herself, but she is such an outstanding example of the essence and activity of this very Tara that my prayer is that the inseparability of Amma and Tara who Increases Power bring even more benefit to millions of beings.

* * *

I returned to see Amma on the last day of her visit to London. On this last day, she offers something slightly different in the evening. It's known as the Devi Bhava Darshan and is where she appears as the Goddess rather than the Mother. She dresses in an elaborate goddess costume and performs her usual hugging, but in this costume and within a golden canopy on a throne, under a golden umbrella. There is a wealth and richness, an overt divinity, that sets this apart from the more ordinary, simple ceremony where she is dressed in a white sari and sits lower down. I don't suppose there is any difference in the quality of the *darshan,* as I truly believe she is inseparable from Divinity the whole time, and there can be no less/more comparison within that reality.

Because I was sitting outside to have a sandwich, I ended up being at the front of the queue for *puja*, which meant sitting right beneath Amma. She began in silence and then began lighting several camphor lamps, circling these to purify the space around her. Then, taking each of the large vases of water in front of her in turn, she closed her eyes and appeared to be meditating on the water. I could really feel a strong buzzing in my third eye every time she did this and have no doubt that something was really happening. The vibration of the water was imbued with her powerful blessing, creating holy water, which was then distributed to each of us.

She gave a short teaching and then led us into meditation and a traditional chanting of *OM* and of the 108 names of the Divine Mother; for me, the highlight, as this pure and powerful spiritual practice made sense of everything surrounding it.

Chapter 13

Global Reach

Tara Protection against Famine

Harare, Zimbabwe

Thursday 9 November 2006

The 12th Tara—Tara Protection against Famine—has gone to Zimbabwe, a country badly in need of help, blessing, and protection. There is so much suffering through poverty, disease, and the oppressive regime of Robert Mugabe.

The friend who has gone to Zimbabwe has been a Tara practitioner for many years and is not afraid to meet and engage with difficulties. Clara is the wife of an Ambassador and someone who has been actively involved in the welfare of orphans and children in Zimbabwe. She will bring a big heart of compassion to whoever she meets. It is very difficult to expose ourselves and be exposed to suffering on a massive scale, and most people, myself included, are somewhat afraid to do so.

To be able to meet it, handle it, and respond appropriately takes a strong and stable mind, the kind of heart and mind that training in the Dharma can give you, but not necessarily straightaway. It can take some time to be truly ready and able to make a positive difference in the lives of others, but to aspire to do this and to do whatever we can is the best approach.

Clara is heading to the Kagyu Samye Ling Zimbabwe, which is in the capital heartlands of the country, in Harare. The Harare Buddhist Centre began informally over 40 years ago, but it wasn't until 1994 that Akong Rinpoche made his first visit and the Centre put down real roots. He was accompanied then by the late Rob Nairn, a former criminologist who was pivotal in introducing mindfulness and the Dharma to southern Africa. Akong Rinpoche had been called the "African Lama" by the 16th Karmapa in what was a prophetic vision of Rinpoche's subsequent influence in Africa.

In recognition of some of the country's unique challenges, Rinpoche had also set up ROKPA International in Zimbabwe, a charity and Support Network that in the early years focused on people affected by HIV/AIDS, and then increasingly on children with disabilities and vulnerable families. It is this work that Clara is travelling to Zimbabwe to support and where she intends to take Tara to.

It is quite shocking to realize how many people there are in the world suffering huge hardship and difficulties: how much disease there is, how much war, how much poverty, starvation, and displacement—things most of us don't expect to experience in the West anymore. Sometimes, the relative comfort of my own life sits uneasily on shoulders that perhaps could bear more of the burden.

Tara Protection against Wild Elephant

Pharping, Nepal

Saturday 18 November 2006

The 13th Tara, Tara Protection against Wild Elephant, has gone to Nepal with my friend Sky. Sky is going first to Bodh Gaya, in India, one of the holiest sites for Buddhists and famous for the bodhi tree under which the Buddha is said to have attained enlightenment. Here she will attend the annual Kagyu Monlam prayers over Christmas.

His Holiness the 17th Karmapa, the head of the Karma Kagyu lineage, has recently taken over responsibilities for leading the Monlam, an international prayer festival held every year on this sacred site. Thousands of people gather together in order to listen to Buddhist teachings and to pray for peace and harmony on Earth and the wellbeing and happiness of the world.

The roots of the ceremony lie in 15th-century Tibet, when the 7th Karmapa established the tradition of great prayer gatherings. People from all over Tibet assembled every year to pray for the benefit of all sentient beings. This tradition was resurrected in India, in 1983, when two great lamas, Kalu Rinpoche and Bokar Rinpoche, spontaneously began holding prayer gatherings at the Mahabodhi Temple in Bodhgaya.

After attending the Monlam prayers, Sky intends to head to Pharping in Nepal, to the site of a very special cave where a "self-arising" image of Green Tara has been slowly emerging from the rockface. The spontaneous arising of a holy image is a phenomenon known as *Rangjung* and it is well documented in Tibet and Nepal. It is seen as the Grace of the deity and supernatural powers are associated with these images.

It is here, where Green Tara emerges from the rock, that Sky hopes to place Tara Protection against Wild Elephant. Significantly, there is a larger image of Ganesh, the Hindu Elephant God, right beside Tara! Pharping is an area of Nepal where both Buddhism and Hinduism are widely practised; and since both Ganesh and Tara represent the "removal of obstacles", it seems very appropriate that they should both be there. Both are credited with great blessing power and people travel from all over the world to see them.

It was in 1979 that a Tibetan lama, Drubthob Rinpoche, first discovered this image of Mother Tara. In fact, he discovered two images emerging from the rock. One of these images has faded, or appears to come and go at least; the other one has become clearer over the years, more distinct and with more detail.

The other strange event connected to this Tara rock image is that on numerous occasions over the past 30 years, she appears to have been secreting holy nectar. Usually the image is dry, but sometimes the rock face will become wet, despite the fact there is no obvious source of water nearby.

Recognizing that this miraculous Tara was indeed a sacred image (and was in fact Tara herself), Rinpoche established a temple around the rock and its image to protect them. He also enshrined statues of the 21 Taras around "self-arisen" Tara. Daily chanting of the Tara Puja is conducted at the temple for the benefit and happiness of all beings.

Tara Protection against Lion

Kerala, India

Tuesday 21 November 2006

Tara Protection against Lion, the 14th Tara, has gone to Kerala, South India, where she will initially visit an ashram with my friend Sarah. Kerala is home to a number of ashrams, including that of Amma, who was born here in the 1950s. It is also a matrilineal society, where mothers are the head of the household. Women have a much higher standing and status in Kerala than they do in the rest of India, and education opportunities are also good. Significantly, Kerala also has more women than men within the culture—again the only state in India where this is the case. In terms of feminine empowerment then, Kerala is perhaps the state that best represents what Tara stands for.

Tara Protection against Snake

London, UK

Friday 8 December 2006

Tara Protection against Snake, the 15th Tara, was an unexpected placement. "Snake" refer to all forms of poison and toxin, as well as snakes themselves and scorpions and other animals whose venom can harm or kill. Within the mind, this Tara protects from wrong views and from dullness of the mind.

I'm working in a pharmacy at the moment and see quite a few drug addicts who are trying to get off heroin who come in for their daily prescription of methadone.

There was one customer, in particular, a young girl, with whom I felt a lot of connection. She seemed very bright and switched on—someone who had a real future if she chose it. She was, however, a known shoplifter, and one particular day came in when the pharmacy was busy and began moving swiftly around the shelves, picking up items, and either pocketing them or putting them back. Shoplifting is quite an art form, and she was a real professional!

The pharmacist confronted her, and she pleaded innocent, got upset and flushed and then left in a hurry. There was no question, looking at the CCTV, that she had been shoplifting. Within the pharmacy, we were all divided as to what we should do. Should she be banned? Or should she be given another chance?

We decided to give her another chance. We would tell her what we knew, what evidence we had, and that we were going to keep a close eye on her, making sure that when she came in, she sat down immediately, within view of one of us, took her medication, and left straightaway. We approached her with this plan the next time she came in. She still denied shoplifting but agreed to our suggestion, and there appeared to be no further problems.

I was surprised to subsequently get an inner message during my daily Tara practice that I should give Tara Protecting from Snake to this young woman—not a particularly easy task, actually, since there were always so many people around and anyway, what on Earth would she think? So I prayed that Tara remove any obstacles to my doing this, if this was indeed her real wish. With the typical speed of Tara's action, the opportunity came in only two days.

That particular afternoon, the young woman came in early, and the locum pharmacist just happened to be out for 15 minutes. Everything was quiet in the shop—no customers, no other colleagues, no one. It was unheard of and really quite bizarre, and I couldn't ignore the significance of this. It was as if everyone "knew" and was playing her part to perfection.

So, with my heart pounding, I took Tara to this girl and said that I had something I would like to give her, if she'd be happy to receive it. She looked surprised, a little bemused, and then read the Tara card accompanying this little statue. She looked at me, smiled warmly and happily, and said she'd love it.

I was so happy! I really wanted to give her a hug, but it wouldn't have been appropriate. I prayed that Tara Protecting from Snake would help her and work with her to overcome her addiction and find a new positive direction for her life.

Tara Protection against Carnivorous Evil Beings

Alaska, USA

Wednesday 17 January 2007

Working with Tara Protection against Carnivorous Evil Beings, the 16th Tara, was challenging from the beginning. The concept of "carnivorous evil beings" seemed much more akin to the vampires of fairy tales than anything I was likely to encounter in ordinary life. Did they really exist? If they did exist, what sort of influence could they have on us, and how would we interact or protect ourselves from potentially malevolent spirits or energies?

Tibetan Buddhism has always had a great respect for, and awareness of, beings in other dimensions, and I had been struck by stories told by other practitioners about Akong Rinpoche's unusual skills when trying to help people with strong mental disturbance. I'd heard that, if someone spoke to him about the presence of other beings in their lives, in their minds, he would always take this seriously, and on occasions even address these beings personally. There were examples of people who might once have been described as "possessed" going to see him and of his extraordinary ability to send these spirits packing, but always with compassion and respect.

The history of Tibetan Buddhism may offer some explanation as to why practitioners accept and actively work with entities in other dimensions. The indigenous religion of Tibet before Buddhism arrived in the 6th century was a shamanic one, known as the Bon religion. Bon is still practised in Tibet today, although is significantly different in many respects from the ancient Bon that pre-dates Tibetan Buddhism.

The early origins of Buddhism in Tibet began with a basket of Buddhist scriptures sent over from India, but these were not translated into Tibetan until a century later. The Tibetan king of this period was Songtsen Gampo (AD 618–649), and it was the influence of his Nepalese wife and consort that sowed the seeds of Buddhism's eventual spread in Tibet.

It wasn't until the 8th century that Tibetan Buddhism became properly established. The Tibetans were naturally shamanistic and animistic in their approach to life, feudalistic in their culture, and often at odds with the very theology and practices of Indian Buddhism. Such was the devotion to Buddhism of King Trisong Detsen (AD 755–797), however, that he invited one of the most powerful Indian Buddhist masters of the day to come to Tibet and effectively help convert the rebels.

And so the great Mahasiddha, Padmasambhava (Guru Rinpoche) arrived in Tibet. He is widely accepted as the true founder of Tibetan Buddhism, using his vast vision, deep compassion, and extraordinary skills to "tame" the wild spirits of the land of Tibet and in the minds of the people, and so lay the foundations for the early Nyingma tradition of Tibetan Buddhism, a tradition that continues to this day.

Tibetan Buddhism might therefore be seen and understood as a kind of fusion between the views and practices of Indian Buddhism and the shamanic, animistic indigenous religion of Tibetan Bon. There are many practices in Tibetan Buddhism, for example, which may homage to the *nagas* (water spirits), fire elementals, and beings in other dimensions.

Within this context then, it makes perfect sense to invoke protection against harm from any troublesome or malevolent beings. Such beings can harm us on a physical level, perhaps through natural disasters or strange accidents, and on the mental level, through imbalances and illnesses that cause depression, paranoia, schizophrenia, and psychosis. Western medicine, and in particular psychiatry, may have a very different understanding and view in our modern world, but there are many cultures around the world where the old ways are still practised, often with beneficial results.

Working with Tara Protecting from Carnivorous Evil Beings opened and expanded my mind. I had long been interested in the shamanic view of life, which was probably why Tibetan Buddhism had been so attractive in the first place. I began to sense the importance of finding a culture, a country, where shamanic influences were still present and where this Tara might be of value.

* * *

With my senses sharpened and ears tuned, I began to expect that the right opportunity would show up in the near future. After the extraordinary series of synchronicities and "coincidences" that were becoming the norm in this journey, I was beginning to understand the power of the mind to manifest. Or was it rather the power of a more meditatively focused mind to be in such natural flow with the universe that the dance between self and other, inner and outer, was blurring all boundaries? Magic became a regular occurrence, as a dualistic mindset and living increasingly dissolved into an everyday experience of Oneness.

Catching up with a musician friend a few days later, I stopped in my tracks to hear him casually announce that he was soon heading off to Alaska. The energy that coursed through my body was unmistakable as I simultaneously recognized this was where Tara Protecting from Carnivorous Evil Beings needed to go.

Jed already had a connection with Tara, and he was such an open, bright spirit that I had no doubt at all that he was the right person for this particular task. He seemed touched to be asked to take a little statue with him, and as I handed her over, I knew that she was in safe hands.

* * *

Shamanism is not typically practised in Alaska anymore, but historically has been widespread in the cold, northern land of what is now part of the United States. Notable shamanic tribes include the Aleut, the Haida, and the Athabaskan, but it was the Tlingit shamans that intrigued me the most.

In the Tlingit culture, shamans are revered as healers and seers. They are dishevelled in appearance, and their hair is regarded as a source of power, and therefore, never cut or even combed. They undertake elaborate rituals, wearing masks and using sacred objects. They often go into a kind of trance when they communicate with the spirits around them, curing sickness by driving out spirits, invoking good weather, and generating good fortune for the fisher folk to bring in large catches.

One particular duty of Tlingit shamans is to expose witches. Witches are powerful men or women who wish ill on and harm others; they are known as *naakws'aati* ("masters of medicine") and are strongly associated with black ravens. The Tlingit shaman is hired to heal the victim from the effects of witchcraft, seeking to find the missing belongings stolen by the witch and cleanse them of any negative energies. As all objects contain energy, personal belongings are regarded as sources of that person's energy, portals to their soul, if you like, and casting spells using a victim's personal belongings can bring sickness and even insanity. For this reason, a shaman's ritual objects are never touched by anyone else, and great efforts are made to ensure that only a natural heir will receive them after a shaman's death.

Knowing that shamanism hasn't been practised at large in Alaska since the 1950s, I didn't expect Tara Protecting from Carnivorous Evil Beings to find her way to a shamanic community or sacred spot, but I was curious where she would land. I had often been struck by the nature of Jed's musicianship. It had an electric quality to it, a charismatic power that built community on the spot and transcended normal cultural or social barriers between people.

* * *

It was to be some time before Jed sent me his account of the journey he took with this Tara, but the sense of completion that came when I read it indicated that she was exactly where she needed to be:

> *Tara has always been the guiding example of open-handed loving-kindness for me since I first heard of her as a teenager. I remember at the time Anna asked me if I would join her project to spread the word and influence of Tara it was a particularly chaotic and free-flowing time in my life. We discussed Tara quite a bit, and I was reminded to focus on open-handed generosity as the best form of protection from negative things. I was planning to take one of the statues to Alaska on a journey I was making there. Somehow, I lost track of this intention in the mix, and I can't remember exactly what happened to the statue.*
>
> *The people I met in Alaska were full of rebellious, joyful energy, carving out a community for themselves amongst that massive wilderness landscape—a great deal of music, dancing, and celebration to keep them together during the dark and difficult winters. I made a very memorable connection with an Inuit lady who told me of the totemic gods of her faith and how they protected the community. Maybe Tara found her place amongst these strong, bright sentinels that adorned the community centre where we played and sang. I hope so.*
>
> *The picture that Anna gave me of Tara has hung above my kitchen table for well over a decade since, keeping watch over the great many discussions and musical performances that bind my community and keep us safe.*

Tara Protection against War

Groot Marico, South Africa

Thursday 8 February 2007

Tara Protection against War, the 17th Tara, is the most wrathful form of Tara. She protects from the darkest, most negative forms of mind and behaviour. Wrathful Tara is black in colour and sits, with hair flaming, holding a phurba (a ritual dagger that cuts through illusion and negativity) directly in front of her heart.

I have to confess I was a little apprehensive about this one. Given that she protects from genocide, black magic, and the worst kinds of atrocity imaginable, I didn't know where this one would lead me. In fact, it has been quite straightforward: She has gone to Africa, with Lama Yeshe, abbot of Samye Ling, and one of his monks, Choden.

As I write this, I remember that I gave my personal *phurba* to Lama Yeshe after I'd finished my month-long retreat at Samye Ling Retreat Centre under his guidance. Lama has been the most wrathful teacher in my life, cutting ruthlessly through so many of my dreams, but ultimately seeking simply to protect me and others from the potential damage of our then feelings and actions.

Looking back, I cannot believe that I was so naive and so headstrong—and heartstrong—but I was. The karma involved in the situations was overwhelming, and I was right and wrong in my view and behaviour. There has perhaps been no teaching more direct or more personal than the ones I received through these experiences and from Lama Yeshe. I went through hell.

At the time I thought that Lama was unreasonable and was putting me through unnecessary hell, but perhaps he just put me right into the heart of the fire that would burn me up in hell, anyway. But despite all the pain and devastation, there was something deep between myself and Lama Yeshe, and eventually, after many years and many tears, a few arguments, and a determined refusal on my part to give up, all the apparent negativity passed away and something different and positive took its place.

So, whilst Lama is not directly responsible for the placing of this particular Tara, it is appropriate that he should be travelling with her. Choden is one of his monks and a close friend of mine, as we shared a cottage in Edinburgh during what were turbulent months for him as he tried to choose between staying a layperson or going back to monastic life and taking robes again. Choden is South African and knows the story of that land and its history well. He also has a strong connection with Tara, and I was delighted to give this Tara to him for this trip. Choden sent this account of the trip on his return:

South Africa was beautiful and abundant. The sun shone everywhere we went, the land felt powerful and space vast. Yet there is the undercurrent of violence lurking in the shadows; those who do not have, envying and conspiring against those who have too much. Fear seemed to be etched onto people's faces.

I took Tara protecting from War to Groot Marico Therapy Centre in the northern part of South Africa. I requested that she be placed on the shrine there. For me, the significance of this aspect of Tara is that her energy and wisdom are like a protective shield, warding off the lurking shadows of greed and violence; they cannot approach or penetrate the light for awareness.

A peaceful healing centre in the African *bushveld,* this therapy centre is bounded by streamss and rolling hills in a pristine environment of clean air, water, and wonderful night skies. Here, there are four streams of activity: healing therapies, environmental preservation, spiritual development, and community service.

Of deep significance for this pilgrimage, the Groot Marico Therapy Centre is where any funds raised on this project will be donated. Akong Rinpoche originally asked if I would fund-raise to build 21 Tara statues for the land around the centre. This pilgrimage began, in part, as a result of that request.

Chapter 14
Healing Taras

Tara Protection against Untimely Death

Holy Isle, Scotland

Thursday 15 February 2007

Tara Protection against Untimely Death, the 18th Tara, is very similar to White Tara, who is not strictly speaking part of the mandala of 21 Taras associated with Green Tara. However, working with Tara Protection against Untimely Death has inspired in me a much stronger and more direct connection with White Tara, and I am now exploring this connection.

White Tara bestows long life, health, merit, and wisdom. She also protects from any opposition to spiritual practice and helps maintain a strong spiritual life.

When I heard that His Holiness the 17th Karmapa had warned that there would be obstacles to his life over the next few years, I was inspired to do traditional White Tara prayers for him. During the session, there then came a strong intuition and wish to do a month-long White Tara retreat for His Holiness.

I approached Ringu Tulku Rinpoche about this, which he positively supported. I then had 10 days to prepare myself and the house for the month's retreat, organizing work to make this possible. It all fell into place and happened quickly and easily, so that is what I'm currently doing!

Like Green Tara, White Tara arose from the tears of Avalokiteshvara, Lord of Compassion. She is perhaps a little more enigmatic than Green Tara, and her practice more likely to be done in retreat than in the household as a daily practice. Sometimes known as Tara who Cheats Death, there are many stories about how she has prolonged life expectancy and lifespan, and it is said that those who fully realize White Tara never die. Whether this refers to maintaining life in the one physical body, or attaining a level of realization that no longer identifies with the physical self and so is free from the suffering within the cycle of birth and death, I'm not entirely sure. I imagine it is the latter.

Having begun this retreat on February 1, I am now just over halfway through. A week into the retreat, I realized that Tara Protection against Untimely Death was directly relevant to this White Tara practice and that, by merging them, the blessing of both increased. So, a couple of days ago, the inspiration to place this Tara came. I intend now to take her to Holy Isle, Arran, where a retreat house dedicated to HH Karmapa has already been built, awaiting the time for him to come and do his own retreat. He has expressed a particular wish to do this, and I hope leaving this Tara statue there will help him fulfil his wish.

Meanwhile, tonight, I start a seven-day period of silence and solitude, intensifying the practice and undoubtedly bringing to the surface more fears and demons for liberation! There will be many White Tara mantras:

Om Tare Tuttare Ture Mama
Aya Punye Jnana Pushtim Kuru Soha

Wednesday 21 February 2007

Retreat

I've just come to the end of the third week of this month's White Tara retreat. This has definitely been the most intense so far. I used to think retreat was a blissful haven, an escape from the world, a time of peace and carefree joy. I think it probably is if you've made a lot of spiritual progress, but for the likes of ordinary samsaric beings like myself, it can be a rough old ride at times!

The reason is that, without the usual distractions of life and because of the purity of the practice—the lineage, the prayers, the deity, and guru's blessing—a great deal of neurosis and ignorance gets exposed!

Happily, this is the very point of retreat, and indeed, of practice, as this is seen as the compost that will mature our minds, but it can get very uncomfortable and painful. The secret is to keep going, trusting that in doing so, all this difficult material will gradually transform into the positive qualities of wisdom, understanding, and compassion.

So, last week, I had to confront lots of difficult, sticky stuff around relationships, and particularly around having children, or not having them. A lot of fear has been surfacing, and I had to go into this fear during my week of silence and solitude.

When examining why I mistrust and fear relationships so much and experience them as confusing and painful as often as I experience them as rich and rewarding, I found a chapter in the well-known spiritual classic, *A Course in Miracles* by Helen Shucman (Foundation for Inner Peace, 1975), which gave me the answer. It put into words the emotional realization I've gradually been having over the years but have not been able to articulate clearly.

It seems that most of us believe in "dream relationships" and seek them out, but as soon as we are in one, or even earlier when we first meet someone we are very attracted to, a whole drama can kick off. This is basically an ego drama. The ego gets very attached to the object of its affection, dreaming dreams of happy futures and security within its "special relationship". The problem is that if the ego's dreams aren't fulfilled—and they rarely are for long or consistently—it can get very angry and upset, and love can turn to hate in a very short period of time, and the "perfect other" is accused, blamed, attacked, and rejected. In short, the ego is not capable of real love at all. It uses another person to prop itself up, and if that other person doesn't comply, there can be all hell to pay.

I see that this is true for me as well, and every time I see it, I know I am harming the other person and myself. It's very uncomfortable to observe and own up to this. It explains a lot of the near insanity that overwhelms many people as soon as the prospect of a "dream relationship" appears.

However, all is not lost! It seems that, although trying to make these dream relationships work is doomed to failure, it does not mean that relationships should be abandoned or discarded. They can be transformed. They can be made "holy". This seems to come about naturally as a result of the spiritual journey we undertake for ourselves, where we seek to overcome the distorting and damaging impact the ego has on ourselves and others.

Through spiritual practice, we come closer to the real love inside, which is not dependent on anyone else for its happiness or peace or security. It is what is there already, and it is something we can then share with another.

To really love is to be secure within oneself, and because there is less ego-need involved, we can be more open to who the other person really is—whatever they do, whether we like it or not. We are less dependent on the other person to meet our own needs. We don't lose ourselves in the chosen other in the vain hope that we will be complete through loving someone else. We are already "found", so the other is always and eternally free, just as we are. These fresh insights helped me come back to a better appreciation of what relationships can and ideally should be.

None of this has, or appears to have, much to do with His Holiness's long life, but again, the fact that these issues have emerged during this retreat has given me more insight into who His Holiness is, too. Whenever any of us do practice and overcome a few more obstacles to our own realization/enlightenment, we are in fact fulfilling his wishes. Having attained enlightenment himself, there is no further need for him to be here for himself, as such. Instead, he is here because of the promise to help all sentient beings overcome suffering and attain realization—the Bodhisattva Vow—which is the best way to alleviate suffering and its causes and help others at the same time.

Ultimately, we are all responsible for our own enlightenment, but with the blessing and help of beings such as the Karmapa, we are able to make greater and more certain progress. In doing this retreat for him, I have come to realize how much more he is doing for me, perhaps without even knowing that I exist. This is humbling and makes me feel close to him.

Thursday 8 March 2007

Heading to Holy Isle

The retreat is complete, and I am on the road again, ready to place the next Tara. The destination is Holy Isle, Arran. Holy Isle is a very special place. Once the home of the Celtic Christian hermit Saint Molaise, it has a long history of spiritual practice and protection. It was bought by the Buddhists a few years ago, after the owner of the island had a vision from Mother Mary instructing her to sell the island to the Buddhists. Remarkably, whilst on retreat in the United States, Lama Yeshe had had a vision of an island of which he would one day be custodian. When he heard about the intended sale of Holy Isle, he visited it and recognized that it was the same island he had seen in his vision! So, Holy Isle is now part of the mandala of Samye Ling, and Lama Yeshe Rinpoche is the director of the Holy Isle Project.

* * *

Down at the south end of the island, the former lighthouse cottages have been converted into a Women's Retreat Centre. The first group of women ever to do the traditional three-year, three-month long retreat recently completed their time, and the centre is currently hosting individuals doing shorter retreats until the next long one, scheduled to begin in 2010.

High up on the hillside above the women's retreat is the cabin built for His Holiness. This is the destination for this particular Tara. En route, I'm spending a little time in Edinburgh, arriving in time for Akong Rinpoche's weekend of teachings, talks, visits, and empowerments to celebrate the 40th anniversary of the founding of Samye Ling. There will be a Green Tara and Medicine Buddha empowerment, which should recharge the spiritual battery in a big way!

Sunday 25 March 2007
Holy Isle

On Friday morning, I placed Tara Protecting from Untimely Death at the retreat cabin on Holy Isle. I arrived on the island on Wednesday, travelling from Ardrossan to Brodick on the Arran ferry, hopping on the bus down to Lamlash and then taking the little boat over to the island.

From Arran, the island is clearly visible, rising up like a great mountain from the water. Protected by its proximity to Arran at the north end, the short crossing to the island takes place on a regular basis during the summer months, but perhaps only twice a week during winter. Volunteers were waiting to greet us, rushing to put down the wooden jetty, but it took a couple of attempts to bring the boat close enough to actually get off at the jetty.

Eight small stupas line the path up to the Centre for World Peace and Health and remind visitors of the Buddhist presence on the island—a presence that is discreet and subtle once you're inside the centre. The island itself is a rare natural haven for wildlife, and a great deal of work has already been done, and continues to be done, to preserve the island's delicate ecology. The centre itself has been designed to have minimal impact on the environment—solar panels, reed beds, organic gardens, and proposed wind turbines all reduce energy expenditure, whilst the planting of native trees and the clearing of invasive non-indigenous plants enhance the original habitat.

The walk to the retreat cabin stretches from one end of the island to the other. At first light on Friday, I set off with Tara in my pocket, listening to the high screech of seagulls as I walked along the rocky path saying mantras and watching the oystercatchers scuttling along the beach, Soay sheep clambering up and down the rocks, and the calm waters of the bay lapping gently at the water's edge. The south end of the island is much more exposed, and in high winds it's virtually impossible to walk that far, but today was calm and mild and there were no problems, except that I missed my footing on one rock and sank deep into mud!

As you approach the south end, you pass a series of rock paintings. First, there is White Tara, then Green Tara, then some of the founders of the Kagyu lineage, namely Marpa, Gampopa, and Milarepa. The lighthouse at the south end comes into view, along with the collection of converted cottages. Beyond the perimeter of the fence, the path turns sharply to the left and begins to make its ascent to the top. A few hundred yards along this path, a small private pathway leads up to the retreat cabin.

Finally reaching the cabin, I turned around and stared at the view across the sea, with just the southern tip of Arran visible to the right of Holy Isle. The sense of space, light, and emptiness was immense; it was absolutely the right place for a meditation retreat cabin. I walked through the little gate into the garden and was amused to see the words "Wisdom Palace" etched into the wood at the entrance to this large but simple wooden hut. Who needs material riches to live abundantly? In truth, it's all in the mind.

Having done three circumambulations, or *koras,* of the cabin, I placed the little Tara in the small stone garden. May Karmapa's life be protected, and may his wish to do retreat here be fulfilled without obstacles when the time comes.

Tara Protection against Sickness

From France to Jamaica

Tuesday 27 March 2007
Medicine Buddha

The Medicine Buddha empowerment given by Akong Rinpoche in Edinburgh recently is timely for working with Tara Protection against Sickness, the 19th Tara. Within the Tibetan tradition, all medicine is created and viewed both spiritually and physically; sickness and disease are said to begin with disharmony in the elements of the body, which is generated through physical or mental imbalance within the mind and/or the outer environment.

The greatest physicians in Tibet are known as *khenpos*, people who have high levels of scholastic ability and accomplishment, often completing up to 15 years of study in Buddhist philosophy before such a title is conferred. Training in Tibetan medicine is additional to this, meaning that a *khenpo* is a highly trained and skilled physician, philosopher, and spiritual adept.

The karmic causes and conditions for disease and sickness are impossible for the ordinary mind to know, but a highly realized master will see not just the display of the sickness itself very clearly but often what gave rise to it in the first place. Any medicine prescribed will often be a combination of physical substances and treatments—herbs, acupuncture, and certain exercises—as well as spiritual practice.

For example, Vajrasattva is recommended for the purification of negativity and its associated manifestations, Medicine Buddha for healing, Green Tara for fear and protection from danger, and White Tara for long life. Any practice that works directly on the mind and how the mind is contributing to or causing that particular imbalance will be advised. Occasionally, spiritually blessed medicine, known as *dutsi,* will be given. *Dutsi* consists of over 100 medicinal herbs ground into dust over the course of a seven-day period, when prayers are recited by one or more realized masters continuously for 24 hours a day.

I am staying at Samye Ling just now, where by good fortune both Akong Rinpoche and Lama Yeshe are in residence at the same time. Yesterday was Medicine Buddha Day, and the monthly *puja* was held in the recently consecrated Medicine Buddha Shrine Room at the top of the temple.

I've not been there before, so doing the practice in a room dedicated to the Medicine Buddha was a happy experience. Amusingly, someone had put my name down on the list of people to pray for, and it was something of a shock to hear my name being read out. So there I was, having been invited to sit with the senior sangha, falling off this illustrious perch into the humbling and strange experience of praying for myself as a sick person!

The Medicine Buddha has empowered my healing work and development in recent years, and this year is no exception. Many ideas and insights are arising, particularly in terms of working with the healing energies of Tara in the future.

Pertaining to the healing qualities of Tara, in particular, a new Tara Healing Garden at Samye Ling is fast approaching completion and due to be officially consecrated in July this year. Around a large central statue of Green Tara are 21 flowerbeds in the shape of lotus petals. Each flowerbed is to be planted up with flowers and medicinal herbs associated with whichever imbalance the emanations of Tara can help correct.

It's tempting to place Tara Protection against Sickness here, but the work with her doesn't feel complete, so I'll continue to do the practice and see where, or to whom, I'm led.

Sunday 1 April 2007

Letting Go

Today has been a teaching on letting go. There is something about Samye Ling that exposes you to yourself, peeling back the layers and sticking pins in the parts you like to keep hidden. Very uncomfortable, and there are times when you feel you could be going slightly crazy. This morning was one of those times.

After a night of interruptions and a lot of wakefulness, I got up grumpy so I decided to go for a morning run to improve my mood. It didn't really work, and by the time I reached Samye Ling, I was feeling annoyed and claustrophobic, aware that people's habits of clinging to each other shuts down life and creates strange control dramas. We can all do this to greater or lesser degrees, often unconsciously and almost always with fear and insecurity at the root.

Whenever I feel trapped by someone else's need or expectation, I get anxious, then confused and guilty, which later develops into resentment and anger and the need to get the hell out. I'm sure there is a psychological term for this problem, but it's come out of some sort of survival pattern. And it's interesting it's coming up around the subject of "sickness", because it feels as if it's an unhealthy pattern and generates mental and emotional stress and unhappiness.

Last night, however, in the middle of the night, I had a strong experience of absolutely not being who I think I am. The memories, thoughts, and ideas of "me, Anna" appeared like wallpaper, creating an impression that seemed to be the truth of who I am but behind the wallpaper there was more—first plaster, then a brick wall, then a huge, empty space. It was a relief, a surprise, to realize that who I think I am is just an attempt to squeeze space into a small shape and hold onto that shape for dear life. Futile!

Nevertheless, coming into relationship with this vast emptiness is a bit scary once you leave the safety of the four walls of "self". You realize that there is no self to protect, yet the self is still there, and it can make its presence felt through various antics. At this point, it might even become psychotic, as the ego-self needs to make its presence felt in larger and more extreme, desperate ways if threatened with "annihilation".

The secret, of course, is to relax and breathe, and keep letting go—letting go of the feelings that are crashing in or the impulses to act that are coming. Keep relaxing into the space of being no one, not who you thought you were. Keep breathing. This seems to calm the fear and allow a greater ease with the dissolution of the familiar self. In truth, it's rather heavenly to feel the neuroses dissipate and the sun come out from behind the dark clouds.

Sunday 27 May 2007

Slow Progress

Finally, I feel that there might be progress with this Tara! Since leaving Scotland and returning south, where I intend to be based again, I've reinstated the healing business I had begun in Edinburgh and am hoping to bring that work to this part of the world.

The work is a mixture of teaching and healing and rests on the foundation that we are already perfect, whole, and complete just as we are, and that it is the blocks to that awareness that need attention. These blocks can prevent us from being our true selves, living the lives we feel are really ours. By using methods that a) focus on this innate enlightened essence and b) dissolve the blocks, positive changes in our experience of life become natural and inevitable.

This work is intended to bring wellbeing and healing to others and protection from sickness. Some "cures" take place in the mind, and in cases where there may be no obvious change to a physical condition, the way in which an individual experiences this condition can radically change, and they can become free of suffering associated with it.

I have recently discovered an inspiring place near West Malling, Kent called The Seekers Trust. It is entirely dedicated to prayer and healing and has been running for over 80 years. It was founded in 1925 by healer and former engineer Charles Simpson, who received channelled guidance from a Doctor Lascelles in spirit. It is an extraordinary story and a true testament to the power of love to heal. Today, they hold Harmony Prayer Circles several times a day, with members of the community coming together to pray for individuals in a small chapel. Individuals also come for healing. They receive requests from people all over the world and rely entirely on donations to continue their work. It truly is a place that testifies to the power of prayer, which I recently saw described as the "science of love".

Wednesday 27 June 2007

France and Beyond

I have for a while sensed that this Tara was destined to go to France. I anticipated giving her to a friend, who was setting out there with the intention of looking for a place to create a healing centre. But there were obstacles in the connection, and in the end I let this idea go.

It seems though that France was indeed on the map for this Tara. I met up with a friend recently who has severe Type 1 diabetes and she's been really struggling. When I heard that she was going to France, I knew that I must give this healing Tara to her. She was delighted and the last I knew at the time was that Leandra was taking Tara to France.

It wasn't until several years later that I learnt the full story of what had happened to this little Tara. Leandra had formed a strong connection to Tara and in her vulnerability at the time, hadn't felt able to let her go. So, Tara had travelled with her through France, then on to New York and Washington. They had then travelled to Portugal, where Leandra met Jamie, the man she was to marry and who changed her life. They had travelled to Turkey together. Leandra had Tara with her at her wedding and kept her beside her bed. She wrote: "I then took her to Jamaica and in true completeness and happiness, I finally felt brave enough to leave her there. I left her on a rocky shelf under a waterfall at Dunn River Falls."

I was so moved by Leandra's story. How much strength and protection she had felt from the tiny statue of Tara and how Tara had accompanied her through her darkest days, supporting her journey into the light again.

Chapter 15
Wish-Fulfilling Jewel

Tara Granting Prosperity
Kensington Palace, London

Tuesday 19 June 2007

You don't have to travel the world to see or meet the world's population!

I've come to Holland Park in an affluent part of West London carrying Tara Granting Prosperity, the 20th Tara. The park is colourful and has managed to pack so much variety into a fairly small area. There's the attractive Kyoto Garden, a *kaiyushiki* (stroll garden); the beautiful flower beds stuffed with seasonal plants; painted murals in colonnades; adventure playgrounds; wooded walks; and open fields.

It's a sunny afternoon, and I notice that virtually everyone I'm walking past is speaking a different language, wearing clothing from another culture, looking at home in a country that is clearly not their original homeland. No one appears to think about this; there is total acceptance of one another—really quite amazing when more than half the world is at war because of the belief that people aren't the same. Here, although the superficial differences that set us apart in some parts of the world are visible, there is total peace and harmony effortlessly.

From here, I walk further into Kensington and arrive at Kensington Park Gardens. It is here that we find the home of the late Princess Diana, who was so tragically killed in Paris in a road accident in 1997.

When I visited the palace, I was struck by a strong sense of the person she was, the life she lived and why her death had such an impact. For many people, she represented an unusual fusion of beauty and innocence, power and fragility, status and ordinariness, and brought a natural compassion and concern to many suffering people and touched many, many lives.

She lived a life of enormous privilege, yet suffered herself and never forgot the humanity of people around her. She may have worn her heart on her sleeve to a degree that wasn't helpful—her heart and anger spilling out at times in public attacks on the Royal Family—and she may have been looking too desperately for love and affection to have maintained stability and dignity in her private life. But she was, I think, a great light in the darkness of many people's lives.

I was struck too by the protection that royal status gives, not to mention the prosperity! Through palaces, status, position, titles, and material abundance, members of such a family are elevated to a degree where ordinary concerns are not the focus of their lives and they are free—if they choose—to be of tremendous service in the world. Whether they take advantage of that or not must depend on motivation rather than opportunity. Moreover, handling such enormous privilege without becoming spoiled, degraded, or indifferent to others takes a level of training, education, and natural compassion that is easily overlooked by those who simply envy the material aspects of this life. Add to that, carrying the projections of so many people and being expected to turn up and preside over so many events . . . well, it's not an easy job.

So, in this very different world, I have come to place Tara Granting Prosperity. I pray that all of us—rich or poor, in terms of material wealth—may prosper in our lives as a result of our qualities and potential to develop ourselves and help others.

Tara Protection against Failure

Edinburgh, Scotland

Thursday 28 June 2007

It's the end of June 2007, and I've come to the end of this pilgrimage, ready to place the final 21st Tara, Tara Protection against Failure. She holds an emblem known as the Glorious Knot and protects from failure in business, projects, agriculture, and failing to implement one's aims. Within the mind, she protects from worry, mental anguish, competitiveness, and indecisiveness. She is the perfect Tara to complete the story and ensure that I get to the end!

Having had such a long, protracted, and uncertain journey with Tara Protection against Sickness recently, it was something of a shock to sit with this one on my shrine, to begin practice, and *whoosh!*, instantly get the message about where to take her: the Salisbury Centre in Edinburgh, where I must put her in the garden there. This Tara Peace Pilgrimage began there 18 months ago, and it is appropriate that, as with all good epics, I should come full circle and end the journey back where it started! There is a wonderful sense of completion in doing that.

Furthermore, the Salisbury Centre is itself undergoing a major refurbishment at the moment, and the placing of this particular Tara at this time will be of great benefit. I feel sure that her presence there will support the many people that come to the centre for spiritual and personal growth and healing; I also pray that this Tara will protect the centre from failure and ensure that it goes forward successfully, to meet its own aims in years to come.

ༀ་ཏཱ་རེ་ཏུཏྟཱ་རེ་ཏུ་རེ་སྭཱ་ཧཱ།

Om Tare Tuttare Ture Soha

21 Emanations of Green Tara

Green Tara is one of the most beloved of the female deities in Tibetan Buddhism. Known for her swift action and dynamic compassion in response to suffering, she is regarded as particularly fearless and is often called on in situations of danger: from external forces or from harmful inner mind states. Green Tara is depicted here with 21 of her emanations: The central green figure of Tara embodies all the qualities and activities of all the different forms of Tara, but each emanation also has a specific function and field of protective activity.

Enhancing Harmony

Protection against
Earth-Caused Disasters

Protection against Floods

Protection against Fire

Protection against
Wind Destruction

Increasing Activities

Enhancing Indestructibility

Protection against Weapons

Protection against Politics

Protection against Thief

Increasing Power

Protection against Famine

Protection against Wild Elephant

Protection against Lion

Protection against Snake

Protection against Carnivorous Evil Beings

Protection against War

Protection against
Untimely Death

Protection against Sickness

Granting Prosperity

Protection against Failure

To meditate on one of the emanations of Tara, visualizing her according to the details shown in the images above, can be a very powerful way to bring her alive in your own mind and life. But do not worry if you find this difficult; the simple intention of making a connection with Tara or with any of her emanations will bring benefit, often in unexpected ways.

White Tara

White Tara is associated with healing, long life, spiritual development, and wisdom. She helps to bring balance to the five elements that make up our physical body and the world around us. Peaceful and beautiful, she sits in full meditation and has seven eyes of wisdom. White Tara sees beyond the apparent solidity of ordinary appearances and recognizes the "emptiness" of all phenomena. The true nature of reality is one of interconnected and ever-changing patterns; realizing this helps to free the mind from grasping to illusory ideas about self and world.

Part Three

Coming Home

Chapter 16
The Fire and the Rose Are One

Undertaking, and completing, the Tara Peace Pilgrimage brought about changes that were not easy for me to describe or even discern at the time, but which are more easily understood now. It is said that through deity practice, when we consciously merge with and become inseparable from the deity, we are strengthening those qualities within us. Green Tara and her emanations represent fearless and dynamic compassion in action. Green Tara also represents protection, and is known for her swift response in the face of danger. She is also known to remove "obstacles" in our lives, whether those be spiritual or material.

Working with each Tara, seeking to understand and embody her qualities and her energy, allowed me to activate those qualities within my own consciousness, and over the 18 months it took to complete the pilgrimage, I gradually became more and more "settled" within my own mind.

The wobbly feelings of homelessness went away and the desolate feelings of grief transformed into more peace, as "finding Tara within" filled me with comfort and renewed intimacy with the Divine. I had completed the project, which was an accomplishment in itself. Prone to bright ideas and initial surges of enthusiasm, I could also easily lose interest in projects or plans and give up rather easily if that happened.

Finally, I had moved back "down South", where I come from and where my family was still living, in such a way that I'd been able to weave the energies of Tara deeply into my own being.

Being away from the support of my teachers, the monastery, and friends on the path, there had been a real danger that I would have ended up lost, confused, disorientated, split, and very unhappy if I'd just tried to return and re-integrate. I'd needed a "process", a gradual return, and the Tara Peace Pilgrimage had been the perfect solution.

It wasn't easy, however, being back in the thick of what Buddhism would call "the samsaric world", in our ordinary society, whose values are a real muddle of greed and compassionate action. I did flounder and had no real idea where I wanted to be or what I wanted to do. I needed a job and a place to live. I was living close to my mother and stepfather at the time, which offered us all a wonderful opportunity to spend time together and get to know each other again, but it wasn't a long-term arrangement.

Then, one day, out of the blue, came an invitation from the chairman of a charity in Oxfordshire: The Abbey in Sutton Courtenay. I'd spent a year there, living in community, several years earlier and had found it both rewarding and challenging. The community was undergoing something of a grassroots revival, having fallen on hard times, and would I be willing and like to return?

Although there were many questions and doubts, deep down I knew this was a kind of "call". I was ready to return, up for the challenge, and grateful to have been offered a purpose that would not only allow me to put into practice all that I'd learnt being away but also provide a context within which to do so: a home, a small salary, and a meaningful project to be a part of.

The Abbey is a beautiful old building set in attractive grounds in a pretty village that connects Oxford and Abingdon via the River Thames, that lovely old river I'd known and whose banks I'd lived on for much of my life—in Sunbury, Henley, Oxford, London, and Sutton Courtenay. It was a friend, and it was at the mouth of this river that I'd placed a small Tara statue back at the beginning of the pilgrimage: Tara Protecting from floods (and attachment). How perfect that I should find myself living once more by her waters.

At The Abbey, despite its Christian roots, the emphasis was on each person finding or following their authentic path. So there was no resistance to what unexpectedly began to emerge as a "new devotion".

I had been so focused on Green Tara during my early years at Samye Ling—probably because of her accessibility and the fact that Green Tara prayers took place every morning in the monastery—that the stealth with which her quieter sister, White Tara, found her way into my life went almost unnoticed. Imperceptibly, though, but with gathering momentum, the more remote and peaceful form of White Tara gradually took up her place in my consciousness and became my practice. When one of my root teachers, Ringu Tulku Rinpoche, suggested that White Tara was my *yidam* practice, I began to understand how natural and how deep the connection with a deity really could be and why this was such a blessing.

A *yidam* is a practice with which we have a particularly strong karmic connection. For the practitioner, a *yidam* is rather like a portal to the awakened mind. It is such a pure and complete embodiment of the enlightened state, for which we have a deep and lasting heartfelt feeling, that our *yidam* practice becomes a very great vehicle for our realization. A *yidam* practice is usually recommended by a teacher, but sometimes chosen by a practitioner through a natural sense of connection or intuitive recognition.

White Tara is associated with the qualities of long life, good health, healing, merit (the accumulation of positive actions), and wisdom. The colour white in Buddhism represents purity and a peaceful nature; White Tara is serene and rests in full lotus position, her mind absorbed in *samadhi* and not caught in the duality of our everyday, *samsaric* existence. Unique to White Tara are her seven eyes: she has eyes on the palms of her hands, the soles of her feet, and one above the brow, as well as two in the usual place. These eyes are variously attributed to aspects of the Buddha's teaching, but in essence, they represent her capacity to see the true nature of reality—to see through and beyond the veils of illusion. They represent wisdom.

As I got to know White Tara ever more fully through her practice, feeling those qualities arising in my own mind more and more, so too, I began to better understand the importance of wisdom in the Buddhist tradition and see that true "holiness", wherever it is found, is always marked by the simultaneous presence of both compassion and wisdom. Indeed, it is said that we cannot ever hope to fly towards enlightenment unless we have the two wings of compassion and wisdom equally alive within our mind.

It also began to dawn on me that wisdom seemed to be represented in many traditions by the Feminine—by Tara in Buddhism, Mary or sometimes the more esoteric Sophia in Christianity, The Mother of the Book (Umm-ul Kitab) in Islam, and Saraswati in Hinduism. She is usually more hidden, seemingly less important for being so, but in fact an equal and vital force within the spiritual world.

On and off the cushion, living in community, my own enquiry deepened, and wordless answers filled my heart. There were times when I felt truly inseparable from White Tara, and many times when my ego got a grip or crept invidiously through fictitious corridors of my mind. But all the while, wisdom really did seem to be dawning.

I saw for myself that the source of all experience was my own mind. That everything that appeared as a thought, feeling, perception, event, another person, my own body; in fact, any form whatsoever, came and went within my own experience; that there was a kind of "stable awareness" that allowed all of this; and that the true identity of the oh-so-familiar "I" was found in *this*, not in the ever-changing events happening at a more superficial level of consciousness. The nature of this stable awareness was clear, translucent, impersonal, yet very intimate and personal. It had no judgements, although it could discriminate and discern distinctions effortlessly, but there was no assessment of these distinctions; they just came and went according to causes and conditions that held no moral or ultimate value.

I saw that at the core of everything that appeared to exist and, in a relative way, did indeed exist (though not in the way we usually think of it) was this "emptiness" that Buddhism spoke about so often and correlated with wisdom.

"Emptiness" seems like a strange term to us, but it refers to the fact that things are "empty" of solid form, independent existence, and individual identity. Their nature is much more akin to particles moving in space in an often-repeating but nevertheless ever-changing sequence of patterns and, as such, they cannot be said to "be", to exist in any permanent or meaningful way.

When we apply this wisdom to the normal content and activity of our minds, we can see how we create a kind of pseudo-reality for ourselves every time we take seriously and make meaning from the many thoughts, feelings, perceptions, sensations, and experiences that constitute our daily life. We can see why we are so often advised to "let go" of whatever is in our mind when seeking peace and so often find it so difficult to do so, for who are we without our stories? What happens to our sense of self without our individual interpretation of events?

This battle between the ego's wish for identity and the true self's wish for liberation is one I think anyone on a spiritual path will recognize. It is usually a long, slow process of loosening the ego's grip and surrendering to the "is-ness" of our natural being, free of the many distracting activities of mind that constantly compete for our attention. We have to become familiar with this "is-ness" and aware of the limitations and problems arising from identifying with the ego as the self.

White Tara was an excellent *yidam* for me, and I noticed a subtle difference in my practice, as if I was more able to go beyond identifying with the form of White Tara herself and sense the big, formless expanse of awareness. I could see that not only was this a much truer "I", or at least the source of a more authentic "I", but that it was also the essence of absolutely everything. I could see this, and I could understand why this would be so. Experience and theology were starting to join up—words on abstract pages in the Scriptures were matched by words rising like bubbles from the depth of the ocean that was my own awareness.

As time went on, I noticed something else: that the searching had stopped, and I no longer had the same sense of burning longing. The "dramas" of my everyday life, and in particular my emotional world, had changed. It wasn't that they had entirely disappeared but rather, they had ceased to grab and control so much of my attention. I could see through them, and although I still got caught up from time to time, I was aware that this was happening—a red flag for me to pay attention to what my mind was up to, rather than believe its version of reality by default and react accordingly.

From the outside, to those who knew me well, it was clear that I was happier. I didn't have all the things that we generally associate with happiness in our culture; in fact, during the 10 years after leaving The Abbey, I didn't have any of them: no home, no fixed job, no relationship, very little money. But my mind was calmer, steadier, more stable, and more peaceful; feelings of loneliness and of "not belonging" were there from time to time. At such times I would turn towards these feelings and just feel them, without judgment, and in that relationship of acceptance, they would invariably transform and my heart would fill with gratitude and the now familiar feeling of "coming home".

Home for me became an inside job. If I could feel at home in myself and practise staying connected to that awareness, then it mattered less and less that I didn't have an external home of my own.

It was curious then that, after leaving The Abbey, my work became that of a companion carer, helping elderly people remain in their own homes for as long as possible. I was privileged to live alongside these people for short periods. I got to observe the many different ways in which they lived in their own homes and helped them continue to do so in ways that gave them comfort and reassurance. I realized just how important home is for so many people, a fundamental and basic need in life, and one that we in Britain work hard to obtain. And yet, I'd given mine up over and over again.

I learnt, once more in a rather acute way, what it means to "live in the present" without knowing what is coming next. There were times I wobbled, but on the whole, over the many years of ending up in fairly extreme situations or circumstances, I learnt to have deep trust, which replaced the terrible insecurity I felt as a child and that had continued through much of my adult life. Eventually, that trust gave way to something even more intrinsic: a quality of "knowing" that I was okay and everything would be okay, even if the worst-case scenario of meeting an untimely death were to happen.

I understood what Mother Julian of Norwich meant when she wrote:

All shall be well,
And all shall be well,
And all manner of thing shall be well.[6]

I understood and resonated with so much of the experience of the people we might describe as "mystics". I wasn't immune from any feeling and could still react in egotistical ways and fall into unhelpful habits, but none of this defined my sense of self, which remained free of all and any attempt to be put in a box of any description.

The more I contemplated, the more I realized that the activation and presence of both the Divine Masculine and the Divine Feminine was the secret of the "holy marriage" that so many mystics spoke about; that when we are able to bring together these two forces, which abide within all of us, in a purified form, something quite extraordinary begins to happen. Carl Jung also identified these forces and named them the *animus* and *anima;* for every woman seeking wholeness, it was essential to "marry" her animus, and for every man, it was union with his anima that held the key to freedom and the gates of Heaven. Wholeness was the path to holiness; wholeness *was* holiness.

* * *

As I write now, on this first day of February 2022, the wind is blowing in the bare trees outside the Poustinia at Hilfield Friary in Dorset. The small wood burner is lit, the candle flutters on the table beside me, birds chirrup, and the smoke from the stove occasionally floats in front of my hut for the day. There is a sense of timelessness within the ever-changing events of time, an inner quiet and stillness so familiar and always akin to the feeling of coming home. I used to locate that feeling in external places—places just like this one—and it's true: it is valued and prioritized in such places. In truth, though, it is everywhere; all of the time, out of time.

Over the many years of seeking, of following the "call", I would invariably recognize this interior quiet when it came as a very personal and intimate feeling of rest, of putting down the world and its cares and coming home.

It didn't matter whether I was in a Christian monastery, convent, or place of prayer; in a Buddhist temple, shrine, or retreat centre; in *Darshan* with Amma or Mother Meera (two greatly revered holy women from India); or in *satsang* with a guru from the Advaita tradition aligned with Ramana Maharshi. It didn't matter if I was sitting on a hillside, in the ruins of an ancient site, by a river, on the beach, in my own back garden, walking in the woods, across fields, sitting on a meditation cushion, standing under the glistening full moon, or watching the dawn light slowly lift the dark veil of the night. When the chattering mind settled down and my true self came to the foreground, it was always the same. Thus, I learnt that there was no one way to God, to the Divine, to the Higher Self; there were as many paths as there were moments when the thinking mind gave way to what lies beyond: pure awareness.

* * *

It had taken over 30 years, but from the original spark of the life-changing dream in which Jesus had shown me who I really was, there had been a journey to discover this for myself, a rich and wonderful journey to know myself as Jesus seemed to know me, to come home.

Finally, I was home. I am home.

Appendices

In the following section, I have included details of ways in which you might begin using some of the practices written about in this book. It is always advisable to seek both initiation and instruction for any new *sadhana* practice (daily spiritual practice) from a qualified Dharma teacher in a recognized lineage. This is the best way to ensure that you are receiving the purest of teachings and can be supported in your development. However, it is possible to start in a very simple way, and this can be particularly helpful if you're new to Buddhism and want to begin practising Tara or Tonglen, for example, in the comfort of your own home.

Appendix I

Green Tara

A Simple Practice for Beginners

Sit comfortably on your meditation cushion or chair. Take a few deep breaths, allowing the mind to settle and open into natural awareness. Then "take refuge" in the enlightened ones, and think clearly to yourself that you are doing this practice in order to benefit all beings. It is important that we train our focus in this way—turning our attention to enlightenment itself (as embodied by the Buddha or other such beings) and our compassionate wish to serve others.

Imagine that everything fades and dissolves into open space. Then imagine that the green seed syllable *TAM* (essence of Green Tara) appears in front of you, radiating light. The *TAM* transforms into Green Tara, seated on an open lotus flower and silvery moon disc. She is adorned in silks and jewels, with her right leg outstretched and her left tucked in meditation posture, smiling and luminous, radiating light in all directions. It is as if she is made of light; there is nothing solid about her appearance.

Imagine then that Tara's gaze falls on you, and, as you feel her love and compassion entering you, your own heart begins to fill and overflow, radiating light. This reaches out to touch the hearts of all the enlightened ones and invites their blessings. It also radiates out to touch and purify all beings, bringing them relief from fear and suffering. Allow your own heart and Tara's heart to merge and to become one.

Then begin to chant her mantra, OM TARE TUTTARE TURE SOHA. Say or sing the mantra out loud for a few cycles and then let it become a gentle whisper under your breath. As you chant Tara's mantra, imagine that from her outstretched right hand comes a river of nectar, which bathes you in turquoise light. This light removes obstacles, whether spiritual or worldly, offers protection, and removes all fear. Tara's fearless compassion and enlightened activity transmit themselves to you, activating these same qualities within, and you begin to feel inseparable from her: You and Tara are one. Stay with this visualization for as long as you wish.

At the end of the practice, imagine that Tara begins to dissolve. First the lotus flower and moon disc dissolve, then Tara herself dissolves, until only the *TAM* in her heart centre remains. This too dissolves, like rays of light being absorbed into the sun.

Allow your mind to rest quietly in this open space. This is your natural and free awareness. As thoughts return, bring your mind to the practice you've just done, and dedicate any merit for the benefit of all beings. Dedication is an important part of any practice as it helps "seal" our positive intentions. It also deepens our compassion and wisdom as we remember our interdependence and ultimate inseparability.

Appendix 2

White Tara Practice

The practice of White Tara is similar to that of Green Tara, but White Tara's qualities and energy are different, and this is reflected in how we visualize her, too.

White Tara is peaceful and serene, sitting in full lotus position, as if fully absorbed in *samadhi*. She has seven eyes, representing her all-seeing wisdom, and brings the blessings of long life, good health, and prosperity. White Tara is a practice we can do for ourselves, which is often done for the long life of our teachers and as an active prayer for the healing of others.

Sit comfortably on your meditation cushion or chair. Take a few deep breaths, allowing the mind to settle and open into natural awareness. Then "take refuge" in the enlightened ones, and think clearly to yourself that you are doing this practice in order to benefit all beings. It is important that we train our focus in this way, turning our attention to enlightenment itself (as embodied by the Buddha or other such beings) and our compassionate wish to serve others.

Imagine that everything fades and dissolves into open space. Then imagine that the white seed syllable *TAM* (essence of White

Tara) appears in front of you, radiating light. The *TAM* transforms into White Tara, seated on an open lotus flower and silvery moon disc. She is adorned in silks and jewels, sitting in full lotus meditation posture, and has seven eyes of wisdom: an open third eye above her two ordinary eyes, two eyes on the palms of her hands, and two on the soles of her feet. She is smiling and luminous, radiating light in all directions.

Imagine then that White Tara's gaze falls on you, and, as you feel her healing love and compassion entering you, your own heart begins to fill and overflow, radiating light. This light reaches out to touch the hearts of all the enlightened ones, inviting their blessings. It also radiates out to all beings, bringing them healing, purification, and peace. Allow your own heart and White Tara's heart to merge and to become one.

Begin to chant her mantra, OM TARE TUTTARE TURE SOHA. Say or sing the mantra out loud for a few cycles and then let it become a gentle whisper under your breath. As you chant Tara's mantra, feel the light and energy of White Tara getting stronger. This light pacifies all sickness and disease, bringing healing, vitality, and all the blessings of good health; life force is strengthened and stabilized. White Tara's long life energies transmit themselves to you, her wisdom penetrates your own mind, and you begin to feel inseparable from her. You and White Tara are one. Stay with this visualization for as long as you wish.

To go deeper with this White Tara practice, you may wish to chant her particular mantra during this period. Traditionally, both mantras are recited; first, the simple Tara mantra and then the longer White Tara mantra:

OM TARE TUTTARE TURE MAMA
AYA PUNYE JNANA PUSHTIM KURU SOHA

At the end of the practice, imagine that Tara begins to dissolve. First the lotus flower and moon disc dissolve, then White Tara herself dissolves, until only the *TAM* in her heart centre remains. This too then dissolves, like rays of light being absorbed into the sun.

Allow your mind to rest quietly in this open space. This is your natural and free awareness. As thoughts return, bring your mind to the practice you've just done, and dedicate any merit for the benefit of all beings. Dedication is a very important part of any practice, as it helps to "seal" our positive intentions. It also deepens our compassion and wisdom as we remember our interdependence and ultimate inseparability.

Appendix 3

Working with the 21 Taras

If you are drawn to work with one or more of the 21 Taras as they appeared in the Tara Peace Pilgrimage, you can do so using a slight modification of the Green Tara practice in Appendix 1. My suggestion would be to become a little familiar with the main Green Tara practice first.

Once you feel confident with that visualization, and have experienced its benefits directly for yourself, you might then wish to substitute the visualization of Green Tara for whichever one of the 21 Taras you would like to focus on.

You would then imagine this Tara appearing in front of you, noting her colour and the particular qualities and energy that she embodies and transmits. Try to really *feel* these qualities, and let them saturate your mind, allowing you to have a definite experience of this particular Tara's presence and blessing in your life. Recite the main Tara mantra as usual, and follow the steps for the practice as above.

Note: It is worth remembering that each colour is associated with a particular activity. So, the colour white represents *pacifying, peaceful activity*; yellow represents *enriching, increasing activity*; red is *powerful and magnetizing activity,* and black is *wrathful and strong activity.* Green generally represents *all-accomplishing activity,* and it is for this reason that we can simply focus on Green Tara and her practice, if we wish, and imagine that everything we wish and pray for is accomplished.

Finally, I also want to mention that there are several versions of the 21 Taras, not one definitive version. The individual Taras will also often have their own specific mantras, but to make the practice accessible to beginners, I suggest just learning and reciting Tara's essential mantra:

Om Tare Tuttare Ture Soha

Appendix 4
Tonglen

Tonglen is a form of meditation that focuses on compassion; on the "giving" and "receiving" of energy in ways that transmute suffering and pain, whether our own or that of others. Its roots are in Buddhism, but it has proven to be so helpful that it is now commonly found in many more everyday and mainstream contexts.

What is unusual about Tonglen is that, perhaps counterintuitively, we are not pushing away suffering at all; rather, we are cultivating our natural compassion and then actually bringing suffering closer. Breathing it into our heart, a heart infused with compassion, we find that suffering is transformed through the power of that compassion, and then returned to the other in the form of healing, blissful nectar.

Tonglen awakens our empathy and compassion in natural ways; it also empowers us to realize that we really can make a difference to another person's suffering, or indeed our own. Whilst this "sending" and "taking" practice assumes one person is sending/giving and another is taking/receiving, it is also perfectly possible to do it for oneself. In this instance, we envisage the "other" as our own suffering self, so our compassionate self is able to send healing to our suffering self.

Example of a Simple Tonglen Practice

Sit comfortably and allow your mind to settle, your breathing to become deeper whilst still being natural. Bring your attention to your breath, and observe the breath mindfully as you inhale and exhale, inhale and exhale. Do this for a little while, attuning to your breathing. Don't worry if your mind wanders off or you find thoughts or emotions distracting your attention; just notice what's happening, let it go, and bring your attention back to your breathing.

As you mindfully breathe, bring your attention to your heart, and imagine that your heart is full of pure white, healing, compassionate light. Notice its qualities of softness, tenderness, and kindness. Allow this compassion to flood your whole being, and have confidence that, with a heart full of compassion, there is nothing that can really harm you, because everything can be transformed. Compassion is the true nature of the awakened heart, and it can purify and transmute all negativity and suffering.

Bring to mind the person, situation, or part of yourself you wish to help. See them in front of you, and feel the contrast between your radiant compassionate heart and the dark energy of suffering and pain in front of you. As you gaze upon them, breathe in and imagine that there are clouds of thick, dark smoke coming from the image in front of you, and this black smoke is being absorbed by and into your radiant heart. As soon as this dark smoke touches your heart, it immediately transforms into bright, white light. Then, breathing out, send this bright, white light of healing back to the image in front of you, and see it being absorbed into that person, situation, or part of yourself. With every breath, repeat this taking and sending cycle, giving and receiving, until there is no more black smoke coming from the other and only light in your own heart, in theirs, and in the space between and around you. Once this happens, the practice is complete.

Allow the image of the other to dissolve into light and disappear. Allow your mind to rest in this natural and open space of awareness, filled with light, for as long as you are able. As thoughts begin to reappear, offer a dedication for the practice you have just done, such as:

> May all beings be healed; may all beings be happy. May suffering and pain cease, and may the causes of suffering and pain cease, and may I and all beings attain enlightenment for the benefit of all.

Notes

Chapter 2: Healing Hands

1 Rainer Maria Rilke. *Die Sonette an Orpheus: Geschrieben als ein Grab-Mal fuer Wera Ouckama-Knoop,* (Berlin, Germany: Insel-Verlag, 1923). Translated from German. Sonnet II, 13.

2 Rainer Maria Rilke. *Letters to a Young Poet,* (London: Penguin Classics, 2014).

Chapter 8: Starting Out

3 Jo Nang Taranatha. *Origin of the Tara Tantra,* (Daramshala, India: Library of Tibetan Works and Archives, 2009).

Chapter 11: I Am Not Just "Me"

4 Marlo Morgan. *Mutant Message Down Under,* (London: Thorsons/Harper Collins, 1994).

5 Neale Donald Walsch. *The Complete Conversations with God,* (New York: JeremyTarcher/Perigee Books, 2005).

Chapter 16: The Fire and the Rose Are One

6 Julian of Norwich. *Revelations of Divine Love* (London: Dover Publications, 2006). First published in 1670.

Glossary

Advaita is the oldest tradition of the Hindu school Vedanta. It literally means "non-secondness" but is usually translated as "nondualism" or "nonduality". It teaches that the phenomenal world, including the body–mind, is nothing more than an illusory appearance, and that knowledge of our true identity as Atman–Brahman, or Witness Consciousness, is the path to liberation.

Akong Rinpoche (1940–2013) was recognized as the reincarnation of the first Akong Rinpoche, abbot of Drolma Lhakang Monastery, in Tibet, when he was four years old. He was a doctor and teacher of Tibetan Medicine and Dharma. In 1967, he co-founded Kagyu Samye Ling Tibetan Buddhist Monastery and Centre in Scotland, the first Tibetan Buddhist Centre in the West. He is also the founder of ROKPA International, an international humanitarian aid organization.

Atisha (AD 982–1054) was a revered Indian master and scholar who went to Tibet in 1042 to help the revival of Buddhism. He founded the Kadampa School whilst teaching at the monastic university of Vikramashila and wrote the first *lamrim* ("graduated path") text, "A Lamp for the Path to Enlightenment".

Bardo is a term commonly used to describe the intermediate state after death and before rebirth. There are, however, several *bardo* states: the bardo of life (which is taught to be no more substantial than a dream); the bardo of sleep and dreams; the bardo of dying; and the bardo of becoming. Each one represents a transitional state of consciousness and is regarded as a powerful opportunity to awaken to our true nature and attain liberation.

Bodhisattva refers to a being who has made a commitment to attain enlightenment for the benefit of all beings (also known as **bodhicitta**) and who works for the benefit of others. A Bodhisattva does not have to be a Buddhist; it is the compassionate wish to free all beings from suffering, together with the wisdom to know how to do this, that is characteristic of a Bodhisattva, who can be found in any walk of life.

Bokar Tulku Rinpoche (1940–2004) was a holder of the Karma Kagyu and Shangpa Kagyu lineages and Heart Son (principal student) of the 2nd Kalu Rinpoche. He was the author of several books, including *Tara: The Feminine Divine* (Clearpoint Press, 1999).

Bon or Yungdrung Bon is the indigenous religion of Tibet. Classical Bon initially developed in the 10th and 11th centuries, but a more ancient tradition of Bon dates from 600 BCE. There is also a more modern tradition, known as New Bon, which began in the 14th century and has elements from both Classical Bon and Tibetan Buddhism.

Brahma Kumaris World Spiritual University is a spiritual organization that originated in Hyderabad, Pakistan in the 1930s. Its founder, Brahma Baba, experienced a series of visions that led him to create a school where the principles and practices of a meditative life could be taught. Today, with centres all over the world, the Brahma Kumaris is the largest spiritual organization to be led by women.

Bruder Klaus, or Nicholas von Flue, (1417–1487) is the patron saint of Switzerland. He was a Swiss hermit and ascetic whose visions compelled him to leave his worldly life and embark on a solitary life of contemplation. As a farmer, military leader, councillor, judge, and family man, he had been held in the highest esteem within his community and is still generally considered to be a model of heroic manhood.

Buddha nature is the fundamental nature of all beings, free from dualistic perceptions and distortions. Buddha nature is inseparable from the nature of Buddha himself; it is our essence and "basic goodness", untainted by any impurity.

Carl Jung (1875–1961) was a Swiss psychiatrist and psychoanalyst who founded analytical psychology. Originally a student and friend of Sigmund Freud, they fell out over fundamental differences of thinking and, after the 1912 publication of Jung's *Psychology of the Unconsious* (Dover, 2003), Freud and Jung began to part company. After a personal crisis and difficult time during the First World War, Jung went on to publish several journal articles and books, including his well-known *Psychological Types.*

Carthusian Order is an enclosed religious order of the Catholic Church for both monks and nuns. Founded by Bruno of Cologne in 1084, the purpose of Carthusian life was total withdrawal from the world to serve God through devotion and privation. Carthusians were solitary contemplatives, living in "cells" (in this case, small, private monastic houses) with a cloister for meditation and a walled garden.

Chenrezig (Avalokiteshvara in Sanskrit) is the embodiment of the compassion of the Buddha. He is regarded as the patron deity of Tibet, commonly depicted in either his Four-Armed or Thousand-Armed form; His Holiness the Dalai Lama is said to be an emanation of Chenrezig.

Chögyam Trungpa Rinpoche (1939–1987) was a Tibetan Buddhist meditation master, teacher, and holder of both the Kagyu and Nyingma lineages. He was also a skilled artist, poet, and scholar who fled Tibet in 1959 and arrived in Oxford with Akong Rinpoche in 1963 to study comparative religion. He co-founded Samye Ling with Akong Rinpoche, but in 1970 moved to the United States, where he became well known for his radical representation of traditional Tibetan Buddhist teachings. He established many meditation and Dharma centres, including Naropa University in Boulder, Colorado, the first accredited Buddhist university in North America.

Cistercian Order was founded in 1098 by Benedictine monks from the Abbey of Molesmes in France, inspired by a wish to return to a simpler way of living according to the Rule of St. Benedict. Cistercians, sometimes known as Trappists, are a Catholic Order of monastic and contemplative monks and nuns living under strict observances.

Darshan is the beholding of a deity, holy person, or sacred object; an experience that is said to convey spiritual blessing on the beholder.

Deity is a representation of enlightened mind in embodied form. There are many deities in Tibetan Buddhism. Some are peaceful, some joyful and sensual, some wrathful. Each deity will have particular qualities they embody, and praying to, or meditating on, a deity (often formalized through a *sadhana* practice) is said to activate those same qualities within our own mind.

Desert Island Discs is a radio programme broadcast on BBC Radio 4. First broadcast in 1942, its popularity continues to this day. Every week, a guest is asked to choose a few items and a selection of pieces of music that they would take with them if they were cast away to a deserted island. They are then interviewed about their lives and why they have made these choices.

Dharma has many translations. It is often used to refer to the teachings of the Buddha (*Buddhadharma*), but in its widest sense it points to ultimate reality, "the way things are". Dharma is the second refuge jewel, literally meaning "that which holds and protects".

Drupchen is an intensive group practice of a *sadhana*, a form of meditation retreat that lasts at least seven days and for 24 hours a day. Drupchens are said to purify the body and mind as well as the environment.

Guru is the term used for a teacher or spiritual guide. It means "dispeller of darkness".

His Holiness the 17th Karmapa, Ogyen Trinley Dorje (1985–) is the head of the 900-year-old Karma Kagyu school of Tibetan Buddhism. Born in 1985, he escaped Tibet in 2000 and now resides at Gyuto Monastery in India, close to His Holiness the 14th Dalai Lama. A skilful teacher of the Tibetan Buddhist Dharma, the Karmapa is said to be an emanation of both Guru Rinpoche (Padmasambhava) and Chenrezig (Avalokiteshvara).

In the Psychiatrist's Chair was a radio programme broadcast on BBC Radio 4, presented by psychiatrist Dr. Anthony Clare. Guests spoke intimately and in depth about their lives and the forces that had shaped them.

Joseph Bazalgette (1819–1891) was an English civil engineer whose major achievements included central London's sewage system. Designed and built in response to the Great Stink of 1858, this system made a dramatic difference to the health and sanitation of Londoners, as well as helping to clean up the River Thames.

Kagyu lineage is one of the four main schools of Tibetan Buddhism: *Ka* means "oral" and *gyu* means "lineage". Known as The Lineage of Oral Transmission, or The Blessing or Practice, its origins can be traced back to the great Indian master and monk Tilopa (AD 988–1069). It is headed by His Holiness the Karmapa, currently His Holiness 17th Karmapa Ogyen Trinley Dorje. The other three major schools are the Nyingma, Gelug, and Sakya.

Kalu Rinpoche (1905–1989) was a Tibetan Buddhist meditation master, teacher, and scholar. He was one of the first Tibetan masters to teach in the West and was widely regarded as a teacher, but controversy came in the wake of a relationship with one of his female students. His reincarnation, the 2nd Kalu Rinpoche (Yangsi Kalu Rinpoche), is currently based in France and is head of the Shangpa Kagyu lineage.

Khata is a traditional ceremonial scarf in Tibetan Buddhism, usually made of white silk, which is offered to teachers as a sign of respect.

Lama Yeshe Losal Rinpoche (1943–) is a meditation master and Dharma teacher in the Karma Kagyu lineage of Tibetan Buddhism. He is currently abbot of Samye Ling Tibetan Monastery in Scotland, the first Tibetan Buddhist centre in the West. After an early adult life of hedonistic living and rebellion, he became a monk in 1980 and went into solitary retreat for several years. In 1992, Lama Yeshe Rinpoche bought Holy Isle, off the coast of Arran in Scotland, for ROKPA Trust and established the Centre for World Peace and Health on the north end and a Women's Retreat Centre at the south end, whilst simultaneously preserving the island as a sanctuary for wildlife.

Mahakala is a male tantric deity and protector deity in the Tibetan Buddhist tradition. There are many different forms of Mahakala, but he is traditionally wrathful in appearance and black in colour.

Mantra is a word or syllable (usually recited in the form of a short string of words) that expresses the essence of a particular deity. The word *mantra* is an abbreviation of two syllables, *mana* and *tra,* meaning "mind" and "protection"; a mantra is therefore said to protect the mind. Protecting the mind from distraction, a mantra focuses our attention and energy on the essence of the deity in question and allows us to experience the "enlightened speech" aspect of enlightenment.

Merit refers to the accumulation of virtue or good actions that are said to result in positive karmic consequences. The greater our merit, the more likely we are to attract the right conditions for enlightenment to arise.

Naga is a snake-like being from the animal realm that lives in or near water. It is commonly associated with fertility of the land, but is sometimes regarded as a troublesome spirit. Appropriate prayers and offerings to the *nagas* help pacify them and transform them into protectors.

National Federation of Spiritual Healers (NFSH), now The Healing Trust, was set up in Kent in 1954 to promote the work of renowned healer Harry Edwards (1893–1976). His vision was for doctors and healers to work alongside each other. The Healing Trust is now one of the largest professional organizations in the United Kingdom, with several affiliated healing organizations.

Poustinia is a Russian word that means "desert". Whilst *poustinias* are often thought of as small, simple, rustic cabins, the actual term *poustinia* refers to the practice of seeking solitude away from the community (often for a day) rather than the place itself.

Ringu Tulku Rinpoche (1952–) is a Tibetan Buddhist master, teacher, and scholar in the Karma Kagyu lineage. He is trained in all schools of Tibetan Buddhism and is a scholar in the Rime movement, which advocates non-sectarianism. He founded Bodhicharya in 1997, an international organization that coordinates worldwide activities to preserve and transmit Buddhist teachings to promote intercultural dialogue and educational and social projects. He is also author of several Dharma books, including *White Tara: Healing Light of Wisdom* (Rigul Trust, 2022).

Sadhana refers to the ritual text of a practice that may require a practitioner to receive formal permission (initiation/empowerment) to practise. A typical *sadhana* will begin with taking refuge and arousing *bodhicitta*, followed by elaborate visualizations of a deity and a period of mantra recitation. This is known as the Generation stage. At the end of the practice, the Completion stage, the visualization is dissolved, allowing the mind to rest in open awareness before a final dedication of merit, to benefit all beings.

Salve Regina is a Catholic prayer and Marian hymn traditionally sung at the close of Compline (the last of the Divine Offices of the day) and as the final prayer of the Rosary. It is also known as the "Hail, Holy Queen".

Samadhi is the state of complete absorption into the Absolute, undisturbed by thought or emotion. Its nature is peaceful, joyful, clear, and alert.

Samsara is the ordinary state of consciousness, the state of suffering caused by "cyclical existence". It arises because the mind is confused and unclear (the state of ignorance) and is driven by the forces of attachment and aversion.

Satsang derives from the Sanskrit words *sat* ("being") and *sanga* ("association") and refers to fellowship with other human beings with similar spiritual aspirations, as well as fellowship with God, or Divine Presence, in meditation.

Seed Syllable represents the quintessence of the deity in one single syllable. In tantric visualization, a seed syllable will appear in open space and then transform into the full embodiment of that particular deity. *TAM* is the seed syllable for Tara, for example.

Sogyal Rinpoche (1947–2019) was a Tibetan Buddhist teacher from the Nyingma School. He established many retreat and meditation centres worldwide and taught widely for 40 years, before stepping down in the wake of allegations of misconduct. He is perhaps best known for his seminal text *The Tibetan Book of Living and Dying* (HarperCollins, 1994).

Songtsen Gampo was the founder of the Tibetan Empire and 33rd Tibetan king, reigning from AD 618–650. He is credited with bringing Buddhism to Tibet.

Stupa represents the enlightened mind in geometrical form. It is built according to a specific design, which incorporates the elements of Earth, Water, Fire, Air, and Space. Its size may vary, but it often contains Buddhist relics. Practitioners will circumambulate larger stupas, doing *koras,* to invoke the blessing of the Buddha or simply focus and quieten the mind.

Tara is a female meditational deity who represents the enlightened feminine aspect. She is also an historical figure, a woman who attained enlightenment and vowed to always take rebirth in a female form. The meditational deity of Tara comes in many forms, but Green Tara and White Tara are the two most commonly practised.

Terma is a hidden teaching associated with the Nyingma school of Tibetan Buddhism and the Bon spiritual tradition of Tibet. *Termas* may be physical objects, such as a text or ritual implement, that are buried in one of the elements (earth, water, air, or space). They can only be revealed, however, through the mind and activity of a *terton,* a "treasure revealer", who has a particular connection with the teaching "concealed" in the *terma.*

Terton is a term in Tibetan Buddhism to refer to a person who is a discoverer of ancient hidden texts or ritual objects (*terma*). Many *tertons* are considered to be reincarnations of the 25 main disciples of Padmasambhava (Guru Rinpoche). Guru Rinpoche and his consort Yeshe Tsogyal are said to have hidden many *termas,* to help liberate and protect beings in a future period that they foresaw as being dark and difficult. That period is often claimed to be our current era.

Thrangu Tulku Rinpoche (1933–2023) is a Tibetan Buddhist master, teacher, and acclaimed scholar in the Kagyu school, the ninth in his particular line. After being awarded the prestigious Geshe Lharampa academic degree in the Gelug tradition, he was awarded the Khenchen degree in the Kagyu tradition. He played a significant role in the recovery of important texts that had been largely destroyed by Chinese Communists.

Tonglen is a traditional form of meditation in Tibetan Buddhism that focuses on compassion. It is the practice of "receiving and sending"—receiving the pain and suffering of others (or oneself) and sending out compassion and love in response. It is a profound mind-training technique that helps to overcome the habitual self-grasping of the human mind, itself the root of all suffering.

Trisong Detsen was the second "Dharma king" and was responsible for bringing Indian teachers to Tibet in an attempt to establish Buddhism. He reigned from AD 755 to 794.

Tulku is the recognized reincarnation of a spiritual master. The process of recognizing a former adept is elaborate, and may involve predictive letters left behind by the earlier incarnation, search parties, and specific tests designed to accurately identify the master in question.

Vajrayana Buddhism. *Vajra* means "indestructible" or "diamond-like" and points to the state of consciousness that remains undisturbed and unaffected by all the comings and goings of the world of phenomena. Vajrayana is the third and most recent of the three main vehicles of Buddhism, and was preceded by the Hinayana and Mahayana schools. Vajrayana incorporates teachings and understandings from both earlier vehicles but also includes *tantras,* the direct path of realization (Mahamudra and Dzogchen), and uses the method of taking the result as the path. As such, it may afford a practitioner swift progress, but it can also more readily lead to egoic delusion and mental confusion. It is seen as essential, therefore, for a Vajrayana student to seek the guidance of a qualified teacher and respected lineage.

Valliscaulian Order was a Catholic religious order founded in Burgundy, France towards the end of the 12th century. It had strong links to the Carthusian and Cistercian orders but was restricted to monks. The order established several houses in France and three in Scotland, but by the 18th century it was failing to attract new novices and was eventually absorbed into the Cistercian order.

World Community for Christian Meditation was started in 1975 by two Benedictine monks, John Main and Laurence Freeman. Inspired by the Desert tradition of early Christianity, John Main felt that the "prayer of the heart" could help spiritual seekers from all walks of life to find a deeper spirituality. WCCM is now a global community united in the practice of meditation in the Christian tradition.

Yidam means "*samaya* of mind" and refers to a practice and deity with whom a practitioner has a particularly close connection; as such, a *yidam* may act as a clear mirror, in which we can see our own innate purity more easily.

Bibliography

General

Howard, Anna. *Death: Breaking the Taboo.* Alresford, UK: Arthur James Ltd., 1996.

Rilke, Rainer Maria. *Die Sonette an Orpheus: Geschrieben als ein Grab-Mal fuer Wera Ouckama-Knoop.* Berlin, Germany: Insel-Verlag, 1923.

———. *Letters to a Young Poet.* London: Penguin Classics, 2014.

Taylor, Allegra. *Healing Hands.* St. Albans, Herts, UK: Optima Publishing, 1992.

Christianity

Harries, Richard, Bishop of Oxford. *Art and the Beauty of God.* Bristol, UK: Mowbray, 2000.

Julian of Norwich *Revelations of Divine Love.* London: Dover Publications, 2006. First published in 1670.

Buddhism

Akong Tulku Rinpoche. *Taming the Tiger: Tibetan Teachings for Improving Daily Life.* London: Rider, an imprint of Ebury Publishing, 1994.

Bokar Tulku Rinpoche. *Tara: The Feminine Divine.* Ashland, OH: Clearpoint Press, 1999.

Evans-Wentz, Walter. *The Tibetan Book of the Dead.* Oxford University Press, 1927.

Jamgön Kongtrul Lodro Taye. *The Treasury of Knowledge.* 10 vols. Translated from Tibetan. Boulder, CO: Snow Lion/Shambhala Publications, 2013.

Jo Nang Taranatha. *Origin of the Tara Tantra.* Dharamshala, India: Library of Tibetan Works and Archives, 2009.

Lama Yeshe Losal Rinpoche. *From a Mountain in Tibet: A Monk's Journey.* London: Penguin Books, 2020.

Pema Chodron. *Tonglen: The Path of Transformation.* ed. Tingzin Otro. Steamboat Springs, CO: The Pema Chodron Foundation, 2001.

Ringu Tulku Rinpoche. *White Tara: Healing Light of Wisdom.* Newton Abbot, UK: Rigul Trust, 2022.

Sogyal Rinpoche. *The Tibetan Book of Living and Dying.* London: HarperCollins, 1994.

Thubten Chodron. *How to Free Your Mind: The Practice of Tara the Liberator.* Boulder, CO: Snow Lion/Shambhala Publications, 2013.

General Spirituality

Morgan, Marlo. *Mutant Message Down Under.* London: Thorsons/HarperCollins, 1994.

Ramana Maharshi and Arthur Osborne. *The Collected Works of Ramana Maharshi.* Rev. ed. Sophia Perennis, 2017. First published in 1959.

Schucman, Helen. *A Course in Miracles.* Novato, CA: Foundation for Inner Peace, 1975.

Walsch, Neale Donald. *Conversations with God: An Uncommon Dialogue.* New York: Tarcher/Perigree, 2005.

Resources

The Abbey Sutton Courtenay
The Green, Abingdon, Oxon OX14 4AF
England, UK
www.theabbey.uk.com
Email: welcome@theabbey.uk.com
Tel: 01235 847401

Bodhicharya UK
www.bodhicharya.org

Findhorn Foundation
The Park, Findhorn, Forres IV36 3TZ
Scotland, UK
www.findhorn.org
Tel: 01309 690311

Hilfield Friary
The Friary, Hilfield, Dorchester, Dorset DT2 7BE
England, UK
www.hilfieldfriary.org.uk
Email: hilfieldssf@franciscans.org.uk
Tel: 01300 341345

Holy Isle
Centre for Peace and World Health
Lamlash Bay, Isle of Arran KA27 8GB
Scotland, UK
www.holyisle.org
Email: reception@holyisle.org
Tel: 01770 601100

Kagyu Samye Ling
Tibetan Buddhist Monastery and Centre for World Peace and Health
Eskdalemuir, Langholm, Dumfriesshire DG13 0QL
Scotland, UK
www.samyeling.org
Email: reception@samyeling.org
Tel: 013873 73232

Marygate House
Holy Island, Lindisfarne, Northumberland TD15 2SD
England, UK
www.marygatehouse.org.uk
Email: enquiries@marygatehouse.co.uk
Tel: 01289 389246

Pluscarden Abbey
Elgin, Morayshire IV30 8UA
Scotland, UK
www.pluscardenabbey.org
Tel: 01343 890257

The Salisbury Centre
2 Salisbury Road, Edinburgh EH16 5AB
Scotland, UK
www.salisburycentre.org
Tel: 0131 667 5438

The Seekers Trust
The Close, Addington, West Malling, Kent ME19 5BL
England, UK
www.theseekerstrust.com
Tel: 01732 843589

The Online Icon Course, Sister Petra Clare
Sadly, Sancti Angeli Skete no longer exists. Sister Petra Clare was received into the Orthodox Church in Shrewsbury in 2015 and spent several years living in a monastery in Greece. Whilst there, she was granted permission to develop an Online Icon Course, which explores the iconography of the Western and Eastern Church through the ages. Both practical and academic, it offers students an opportunity to learn from Sister Petra Clare's in-depth knowledge of this subject. For more information, visit East X West at www.exw-onlineiconcourse.org

Acknowledgements

In many ways, this book is the culmination of experiences and reflections made possible because of the truth of interdependence. Nothing I have done, thought, or felt has happened in isolation. There are so many people who have helped to shape all I have written and shared in this book, and they are all worthy of acknowledgement.

I have dedicated this book to my late mother and father. Sadly, my mother died shortly before I finished writing this book, but she had read much of it. Having lived through many of my ups and downs, she often commented on how much she had seen me change. This convinced her that my unconventional choices may well have been justified, though it was only when I finally settled into a home and got an "ordinary" job that she believed she'd done her job as a mother!

My father died many years ago, but to some extent it was his years of living with a terminal diagnosis that galvanized my motivation to study Buddhism and its deep wisdom about death and dying. Dad encouraged creativity and learning and was proud of my accomplishments at university and in broadcasting. I consider myself very fortunate to have had two parents who loved me, whom I also loved. We certainly had our challenges along the way, but we always bounced back, and I look back with a heart full of gratitude for everything we shared.

At this point, I have to mention my brother, Rupert Howard. He has been my rock and best friend, a rare combination of warmth, emotional intelligence, and practical wisdom. He arrived when I was nearly three years old, his tiny feet and toes proof that he was real. I cannot thank him enough for all the love, kindness, laughter, and support he's given me over the years. He, his wife Rachael, and my two nephews, Charlie and Alex, are the best family anyone could hope for.

I would like to also thank my stepfather, Allan Thomson, for his unwavering support over the many years he has been there. A natural sceptic as a scientist, he has asked questions, challenged beliefs, refuted dogmas, and resisted theories "without evidence". But nonetheless, his interest in Buddhism grew, and his enquiring mind and compassionate heart found answers that science cannot (yet) explain. When he came into my life, he came with two wonderful sons: Simon and Jeremy. Simon sadly died in 2016, in his early 50s, after a long struggle with heroin addiction. One of the kindest men, he was a true brother, never to be forgotten.

And then there's my inspiring, elegant, fun-loving stepmum, Juliet. She brought my father great joy and looked after him with such devotion and care for the last years of his life. If I'm as spirited as she is in my late 80s, it'll be her influence rubbing off! She too came into my life with two wonderful sons: Simon and Alastair.

I also want to acknowledge a particular person who played an important role in my life. Shirley du Boulay was a writer whom I first met when I interviewed her for BBC Radio Oxford. Author of many spiritual biographies, from Teresa of Avila to Swami Abhishiktenanda, she embraced Western and Eastern spirituality and advocated meditation as the path to include, and transcend, all apparent differences. She taught me to meditate, introduced me to the editor of my first solo book, *Death: Breaking the Taboo,* and understood what it meant to love a monk, as she had fallen in love with, and eventually married, a Jesuit priest. Over the 30 years I knew her, her mentoring and friendship encompassed literary, spiritual, professional, emotional, relational, and practical support. She was my "spiritual aunt", and I owe her so much.

This book could not have been written without the extraordinary presence of certain spiritual teachers in my life—in particular, my "root gurus": Akong Tulku Rinpoche, Lama Yeshe Losal Rinpoche, and Ringu Tulku Rinpoche. My gratitude to them can never be measured, but if one day I should indeed fully recognize and stabilize in enlightenment, it will be in large part due to their kindness, the inspiration and example of their own lives, and their teaching. I owe grateful thanks as well to the late Chögyal Namkhai Norbu, as well as Mingyur Dorje Rinpoche and, from a more advaita-oriented tradition, Satyananda.

Nor could it have been written without my dear friend Yangdak. We met and fell in love when he was a Buddhist monk, a relationship that tore us apart and caused many difficulties. After many years with no contact we met again, and so began a very precious friendship that continues to this day. My relationship with Mikki also survived the devastation of our then dreams. We stayed friends, and the day he married "the right woman" was a happy one for everyone at the monastery.

There are many other friends who have made a direct contribution to this book by supporting the Tara Peace Pilgrimage in its mission to send small statues to places in need around the world. They are Emma Fenwick, Rob Parry, Sara Trevelyan, Natalya Afanasyeva, Choden, Jed Milroy, Justin and Lizzy Nimmo, Sarah Mahoney, Sky, and Leandra Green. Many of these friends have written short pieces, describing their experience, and these form an important part of the text of this book. Thank you also to Vin Harris, whose memories of the early days of Samye Ling shone a light on years I missed.

I would also like to thank the many other friends who have been with me on this journey we call Life and whose support with this book has been invaluable. They are David Clargo, Clara Coogan, Karen Errington, Martin Field, Mary Heneghan, Gil Hilleard, Gaby Hock, David Hughes, my late friend Debbie Jedwab, Rachel Lebus, Lolai O'Dwyer, Martine Postel, Peter Rhodes-Dimmer, Ray Stubb,

Stephen Wheatley, Carmen White, Diane Zervas-Hirst, Alessandra Zwerger, and so many more.

Thank you, too, to Wendy Yorke, whose tireless energy, boundless positivity, professionalism, and sheer hard work as my agent has got me this far. She dragged me, sometimes quietly kicking and screaming, from the peaceful cave of anonymity into a busier marketplace, to allow this book to reach those for whom it might serve as a light along the way.

Enormous thanks also go to Sabine Weeke, Editorial Director of Findhorn Press, who took the plunge and decided to publish this book. It has been a joy to work with her, with the Editor, Nicky Leach and with the entire team of Findhorn Press and Inner Traditions International.

Illustrations

We gratefully acknowledge the artist of the Tara illustrations for their work. The illustrations were sourced at: *www.pinterest.co.uk/kariaudarsvansson/nyingma-lama-longchenpa*. Every effort has been made by the author to ascertain the artist's name; please contact the publisher if you can provide more information.

About the Author

Photo by André de Smet

Anna Howard's career began in 1989 when she joined BBC Radio Oxford as a Programme Assistant. She worked on the daily book programme, selecting newly published books for review and liaising with authors and/or publishers for interviews. In 1991, she became a broadcaster, producing and presenting a number of documentaries. A graduate of Oxford University, with a degree in Psychology, Anna has a particular interest in mental health, social care, and general wellbeing. Programmes she produced on Alzheimer's disease, forensic psychiatry and a documentary about young lifers from Aylesbury Young Offenders Institute earned her a reputation for insightful, honest, and revealing interviewing. From 1994 onwards, she produced and presented a weekly programme called *My Life*, where she conducted in-depth interviews with local people about their lives and musical interests.

In 1995, Anna worked alongside author and photographer Jon Davison on his book *Oxford: Images and Recollections.* Published by Blackwell's, it immediately sold more than 10,000 copies, going on to become a bestseller. A year later, Anna produced her own first book, a collection of reminiscences about death entitled *Death: Breaking the Taboo* (Arthur James, 1996), following a personal and ultimately healing experience with death. She interviewed a variety of people, from mystics to murderers, all of whom spoke candidly and openly about their experiences.

In 1997, she moved to Scotland to live at Samye Ling Tibetan Buddhist Monastery and the next 10 years were largely devoted to the study, practice, and application of Tibetan Buddhism. During this period, she joined the editorial team of *The Good Retreat Guide* (Stafford Whiteaker, Rider, 2004) for the fifth edition of the guide, visiting and reviewing retreat centres around the country.

In 2004, she began teaching meditation under the guidance of Buddhist teachers and offering talks and workshops to introduce newcomers to Tara, a female embodiment of wisdom and compassion within the Tibetan Buddhist tradition. In 2016, this work expanded when she joined forces with friend and colleague Dean Carter in Dorset. Together, they offer a body of White Tara work through the Centre for Pure Sound and through White Tara Healing and Meditation.

Anna can be contacted via her website:

www.white-tara.co.uk

Also of Interest

Sage, Huntress, Lover, Queen

Access Your Power and Creativity through Sacred Female Archetypes

by Mara Branscombe

Guiding you to awaken the wisdom of your feminine soul, Mara Branscombe presents an inspiring look at the seven feminine archetypes that prevail in the modern psyche. Explore each archetype's beneficial qualities and shadow aspects, and be inspired to deeply embody each archetype and activate a life of fulfilment and happiness. With creative practices, mind-body rituals, and guided visualizations.

ISBN 9-781-64411-793-4